S0-DYS-717

Beer is Good.

If centuries of existence are not enough to prove that fact, just listen to your taste buds. They'll tell you beer is good, and they've probably already led you to your favorite beer styles, breweries, and brands.

Those taste buds, however, are about to experience the magic that happens when great beer is served with great food. New flavors emerge, ingredients coexist, and the palate grows.

By combining classic styles with both traditional and innovative recipes, this book will help you discover a brand new world of beer. Together, a perfect beer and food duo is unstoppable. Use the pairings to increase your own knowledge of great beer, delight dinner guests, or help you order up the best combination the next time you're dining out.

Start experimenting today. Your taste buds will thank you.

Copyright © 2008 CQ Products
Waverly, IA 50677
All rights reserved.
No part of this book may be reproduced or transmitted in any form
or by any means, electronic or mechanical, including photocopying,
recording or by any information storage and retrieval system, without
permission in writing from the publisher.

Printed in the United States of America
by G&R Publishing Co.

Distributed By:

507 Industrial Street
Waverly, IA 50677

ISBN-13: 978-1-56383-297-0
ISBN-10: 1-56383-297-6
Item #7090

Table of Contents

Food Rules

The key to finding a good beer and food pairing is to be open to suggestion. Since taste is subjective, what works for one person may not work for another. If you like a certain pairing, go for it! Here are a few general, but not strict, rules to follow:

- The more hop bitterness a beer has, the heartier the meal needs to be. Try to achieve a balance for the palate, without either component being too overwhelming.
- Generally, keep sweet foods with sweeter beers and tart or bitter foods with bitter beers. An exception to this rule is when serving dry, robust beers with sweet chocolates and desserts.
- Experiment with both contrasting and complementary pairings. Sometimes an opposite flavor is the best choice in order to balance a strong component, and other times a similar flavor is desired in order to enhance a component. Don't be afraid to play around with both types of pairings.

Beer & Cheese

Doesn't wine go with cheese? Yes, wine and cheese have been grouped together for ages. But did you know beer and cheese pairings date back to the Middle Ages? Belgium monasteries, then and now, are known for their exceptional beers and cheeses. In fact, a beer and cheese pairing is often more desirable than wine and cheese because the overpowering acidity in wine can ruin the pleasurable taste of the cheese. Beer and cheese, however, have similar origins. They complement each other by sharing comparable characteristics in both aroma and flavor.

Hold a Tasting

One of the best things about discovering a great beer and food pairing is sharing that experience with others. A great way to do this is to hold a tasting. Don't worry about not knowing enough about the beer; all you need to know is what you like.

- A tasting can be as simple as having several brands of a certain beer style with a few appetizers, or as grand as serving several beer styles, each with complementing foods.
- Offer bottled water for guests to rinse their palate between tastings.
- Pour small samplings: all you need is 2 to 3 ounces of each beer per person.
- Offer appropriate foods using inspiration from the recipes in this book.
- Keep it fun without being snooty. Remember: it's all about what tastes good to you!

Beer Glassware

Though beer can be tasty in almost any mug or glass, the flavors, carbonation, and frothy head of certain beers are enhanced when served in the proper glassware.

Weizen Glass

Hefeweizen
Dunkel Weizen
American Wheat Ale

Stange

Lambic
Rauchbier
Fruit Beer

Stein

Traditional Bock
Doppelbock
Dry Stout

Tumbler

Witbier or White Ale
Belgian Strong Ale
Gueuze Lambic

Flute

Maibock
Eisbock

Footed Pilsner

Pilsener
Light Lager
Dortmunder
Low or No Alcohol Beer

Stem Glass

Porter
Robust Porter
Doppelbock

Shaker Pint

Summer Ale
India Pale Ale
Amber Ale or Lager

Thistle

Scotch Ale or Wee Heavy
Bière de Garde
Saison/Farmhouse Ale

Lager Glass

Lager
Hard Cider
California Common

Snifter

Barley Wine Ale
Imperial Stout
Quadrupel
Traditional Mead

English Pint

Golden or Blonde Ale
Pale Ale
Brown Ale
Sweet or Oatmeal Stout
Pumpkin Ale

Dimpled Mug

Oktoberfest or Märzen
Dark Lager
Herbed or Spiced Beer
Cream Ale

Terms to Know

Adjunct – fermentable material used as a substitute for traditional grains to make beer lighter-bodied or cheaper

Alcohol by Volume – the amount of alcohol in beer measured in terms of percentage volume of alcohol per volume of beer

Ale – beers distinguished by use of top fermenting yeast strains, which perform at warmer temperatures than yeasts used to brew Lager beer. The byproducts of top fermenting yeast have a more evident taste and aroma. Fruitiness and esters are often part of an Ale's character

Bitter – refers to the bitterness of hops or malt husks. The sensation is noted on the back of the tongue

Bitterness – the perception of bitter flavor derived from hops

Body – thickness and mouth-filling property of a beer. It is often described as full- or thin-bodied

Carbonation – the sparkle and bubbles in beer caused by carbon dioxide. It is either created during fermentation or injected later

Dry-hopping – the addition of dry hops to fermenting or aging beer, used to increase hop character and aroma

Fermentation – the conversion of sugars into ethyl alcohol and carbon dioxide, through the action of yeast

Hops – an herb added to boiling wort or fermenting beer to impart a bitter aroma and flavor. *Hoppy or Hoppiness* is the flavor or aroma of hops, but not including hop bitterness

Lager – beers distinguished by use of bottom fermenting yeast strains at colder fermentation temperatures than Ale beer. The cooler environment inhibits the natural production of esters and other byproducts, resulting in a crisper tasting beer

Malt – the foundation ingredient in beer

Malting – the process by which barley is steeped in water, germinated, then kilned to convert insoluble starch to soluble substances and sugar

Mouthfeel – a sensation derived from the consistency or density of a beer, often described as thin or full

Secondary fermentation – the stage of fermentation occurring in a closed container for several weeks to several months

Shelf life – the number of days a beer will retain its peak drinkability. The shelf life of most commercially produced beers is usually a maximum of four months.

Sour/Acidic – vinegar-like or lemon-like flavors or aroma of beer

Sweet – the taste of sugar in beer; experienced at the front of the tongue

Yeast – a micro-organism of the fungus family; an ingredient in beer

Beer Combos

The many flavors and styles of beer have inspired adventurous drinkers to create beer combinations. Try these popular blends, or get creative and make your own! Always pour the lighter beer first.

Black & Tan =	1 part Porter or Stout + 1 part Pale Ale
All Irish Black & Tan =	1 part Guinness Stout + 1 part Smithwick's Irish Ale
Black & Blue =	1 part Guinness + 1 part Blue Moon
Black & Gold =	1 part Stout + 1 part Hard Cider
Black & Orange =	1 part Stout + 1 part Pumpkin Ale
Bee Sting =	1 part Amber Ale + 1 part honey-flavored beer
Belgian Brunette =	1 part Guinness + 1 part Stella Artois
Berry Black =	1 part Dark Lager + 1 part Fruit Beer
Chocolate-Covered Cherry =	1 part Chocolate Stout + 1 part Fruit Lambic
Eclipse =	1 part Stout + 1 part White Ale
Half & Half =	1 part Stout + 1 part Lager
Midnight =	1 part Guinness + splash of Port
Octoberry =	1 part Oktoberfest + 1 part Fruit Lambic or berry-flavored beer
October Sky =	1 part Dark Lager + 1 part Oktoberfest
Red Sunset =	1 part Amber Ale + 1 part Hefeweizen
Red Apple =	1 part Hard Cider + 1 part Amber Ale
Red-Nosed Black Bear =	1 part Leinenkugel's Creamy Dark + 1 part Leinenkugel's Berry Weiss + 1 part Leinenkugel's Red Lager
Shandy =	1 part Guinness + 1 part lemon lime soda
Snakebite =	1 part Hard Cider + 1 part Lager or Guinness

White Ale or Witbier

Belgian-style White Ale, Witbier, or simply Witte, is very pale in color and brewed using unmalted wheat and malted barley. The flavors of coriander and orange peel often spice the beer. White Ale is served cloudy, due to suspended yeast and wheat proteins that cause the beer to look hazy and white when cold, hence the name.

White Ale • Witbier

Try it

Allagash White
Allagash Brewing Company

Blanche de Brooklyn
Brooklyn Brewery

Blue Moon Belgian White Ale
Blue Moon Brewing Company

Calabaza Blanca
Jolly Pumpkin Artisan Ales

Celis White
Michigan Brewing Company

Double White Ale
Southampton Publick House

Hoegaarden Original White Ale
Brouwerij van Hoegaarden

Holy Moses White Ale
Great Lakes Brewing Company

Little White Lie
Russian River Brewing Company

Mothership Wit
New Belgium Brewing Company

Ommegang Witte Ale
Brewery Ommegang

Red & White
Dogfish Head Craft Brewed Ales

St. Bernardus Witbier
Brouwerij St. Bernardus

Whirlwind Witbier
Victory Brewing Company

ZŌN
Boulevard Brewing Company

Serve at 40-45° F
Serve in Basic Tumbler or Stange

Serve with

A classic dish to serve with White Ale is steamed mussels.
The beer also complements lighter seafood dishes and
light cheeses, such as mascarpone or white herbed cheese.
For dessert, orange and lemon flavors make a great match.

Classic Steamed Mussels

Less is more when it comes to cooking mussels. Use only fresh mussels that are tightly closed when purchased, and prepare them right away. Mussels are traditionally steamed in water or white wine, but steaming them in White Ale enhances the taste of the beer with which they are served.

1½ to 4½ lbs. mussels
1 C. water, white wine, or
    White Ale

Clean mussels by scrubbing them thoroughly with a brush under cold water. Discard any chipped, open, or cracked mussels. Pour liquid into a 4- to 6-quart pot over medium-high heat. The liquid will only cover the bottom of the pot. Bring liquid to a boil, then carefully dump mussels into pot and cover. Reduce heat to medium and cook, stirring occasionally, until mussels open, about 3 to 6 minutes. Scoop out mussels with a slotted spoon, discarding any that are unopened. Transfer mussels to a serving bowl. The mussels should be picked from their shells with a fork and eaten. Or, use two connected halves of a shell as a utensil to pick out mussels and scoop them into your mouth. Place a small bucket or bowl on the table for discarding shells.

Olive & Herb Cream Spread

This recipe can be used as a spread for water crackers or thin wafers. Or, spread over flour tortillas, roll up, and cut into 1″ pieces. Secure each piece with a toothpick.

2 (3 oz.) pkgs. cream cheese,
  softened
1 (6 oz.) can pitted black
  olives, drained and chopped
1 (5 oz.) jar pitted green
  olives, drained and chopped

3 T. chopped fresh parsley
½ tsp. crushed red pepper
  flakes
Salt and pepper to taste
2 T. sesame seeds

In a medium bowl, beat cream cheese until smooth and creamy. Mix in olives, parsley, and red pepper flakes; season to taste with salt and pepper. Spoon mixture into a serving bowl and sprinkle sesame seeds over top.

Broiled Halibut
with Lemon and Dill

This light and lemony seafood dish is the perfect complement for a White Ale.

¼ C. extra-virgin olive oil,
  divided
1 (2 lb.) halibut fillet
1 large lemon, quartered

1 tsp. sea salt
1 tsp. garlic powder
1 T. dillweed

Preheat oven broiler and coat a baking sheet or broiling pan with olive oil. Rinse fillet and pat dry with paper towels. Place fillet on pan and brush with additional oil. Squeeze lemon wedges over fillet and season generously with sea salt, garlic powder, and dillweed. Broil for 15 to 20 minutes, or until fillet turns opaque and flakes easily with a fork. Transfer fillet to a platter and cut into pieces to serve.

Lemon Panna Cotta

A traditional Italian custard, Panna Cotta comes to life with the citrus flavors of lemon and orange.

⅓ C. milk
1 (0.3 oz.) box sugar-free
  lemon gelatin powder
2½ C. heavy cream

½ C. sugar
1½ tsp. vanilla extract
Finely grated orange peel

In a small bowl, gently combine milk and lemon gelatin powder; set aside. In a medium saucepan over medium heat, combine cream and sugar. Bring to a full boil and pour gelatin mixture into cream, stirring until completely dissolved. Cook for 1 minute, stirring constantly. Remove from heat and stir in vanilla. Pour liquid into six individual ramekins; let cool to room temperature. Once cooled, cover dishes with plastic wrap and refrigerate for at least 4 hours or overnight. Invert custard onto dessert dishes and garnish each serving with a little grated orange peel.

Traditionally, a stein is a stone version of a beer mug with a lid. The use of steins dates back to the Black Plague to prevent flies from dropping in one's drink.

Golden & Blonde Ale

Golden or Blonde Ale of North American origin has a crisp, dry palate, light to medium body, and light malt sweetness. It is straw to golden blonde in color and may have a low to medium hop floral aroma.

Golden Ale • Blonde Ale

Try it

Bailey's Ale
Cisco Brewers

Beach Bum Blonde Ale
Anheuser-Busch

Clipper City Gold Ale
Clipper City Brewing Company

Demolition
Goose Island Beer Company

Drawbridge Blonde
Hale's Ales Brewery

Fireman's #4 Blonde Ale
Real Ale Brewing Company

Golden Ale
The St. George Brewing Company

Hell's Belle Belgian Blond
Big Boss Brewing Company

Oregon Golden Ale
Rogue Ales

Pete's Wicked Rally Cap Ale
Pete's Brewing Company

Rapscallion Premier
Concord Brewery

Redhook Blonde
Redhook Ale Brewery

Skinny Dip
New Belgium Brewing Company

Sparkling Ale
Coopers Brewery

Third Coast Beer
Bell's Brewery, Inc.

Serve at 40-45° F
Serve in English Pint

Serve with

Pair a Golden or Blonde Ale with lighter food, such as greens, chicken, or fish. Classic cheeses to serve are Monterey Jack, brick, or other light and nutty cheeses. Just as with White Ale, the flavors of orange and lemon highlight the palate of a Golden or Blonde Ale.

Seared Ahi Tuna

A floral Blonde Ale nicely complements this dish.

1 green onion, thinly sliced, divided
2 T. dark sesame oil
2 T. soy sauce
1 T. grated fresh gingerroot
1 clove garlic, minced
1 tsp. lime juice
2 (6 to 8 oz.) ahi tuna steaks, ¾″ thick

Set aside some green onion slices for garnish. In a small bowl, combine remaining green onions, oil, soy sauce, gingerroot, garlic, and lime juice. Pour dressing into a large zippered plastic bag and add tuna steaks; seal and refrigerate for at least 1 hour. Place a non-stick skillet over medium-high heat. When pan is hot, remove tuna steaks from marinade and sear them for 1 to 3 minutes on each side, or to desired doneness. Discard marinade. Remove tuna from pan and slice into ¼″ thick pieces. Serve over white rice, lettuce, or fennel salad. Sprinkle with reserved green onions.

Citrus Salad
with Grilled Chicken

Grilled chicken and this sweet vinaigrette are the perfect balance for a Golden or Blonde Ale.

½ C. orange juice
¼ C. lime juice
2 shallots, minced
2 cloves garlic, minced
1 tsp. chili powder
1 tsp. ground cumin
1 tsp. sugar
4 skinless, boneless chicken breast halves
8 C. torn romaine lettuce
2 oranges, peeled, segmented, and chopped
2 stalks celery, sliced
4 green onions, chopped

In a small bowl, whisk together orange juice, lime juice, shallots, garlic, chili powder, cumin, and sugar. Pour half of the dressing into a large zippered plastic bag and add chicken breast halves; seal and refrigerate for at least 2 hours. Refrigerate remaining dressing. Preheat an outdoor grill to medium-high heat and lightly oil the grate. In a large bowl, toss together lettuce, oranges, celery, and green onions; set aside. Place chicken on grill; discard marinade. Cook for 6 to 8 minutes on each side, or until chicken juices run clear. Slice grilled chicken into thin strips. Drizzle reserved dressing over salad; toss and top with sliced chicken.

Chicken Monterey

White wine is traditionally used in this recipe, but a Golden or Blonde Ale makes a terrific substitute and highlights the flavor of your beer.

4 T. butter, divided
¼ C. chopped onion
4 large mushrooms, chopped
1 small clove garlic, minced
½ C. plus 1 T. flour, divided
¼ C. chicken broth
½ tsp. celery salt

¼ tsp. white pepper
¼ C. Golden or Blonde Ale
¾ C. shredded Monterey
    Jack cheese, divided
Salt and pepper to taste
4 skinless, boneless chicken
    breast halves

Preheat oven to 300°. Melt 2 tablespoons butter in a medium skillet over medium heat. Stir in onion, mushrooms, and garlic; sauté until tender, about 10 minutes. Stir in 1 tablespoon flour, chicken broth, celery salt, white pepper, and Ale. Reduce heat to low and cook, stirring frequently, until thickened. Mix in ½ cup cheese and stir until melted. In a shallow bowl, combine remaining flour with salt and pepper. Dredge chicken in flour until evenly coated. Melt remaining butter in a large skillet over medium-high heat. Cook chicken until browned on all sides. Transfer chicken to a lightly greased medium baking dish; cover with sauce. Sprinkle remaining cheese over top. Bake, uncovered, until chicken is no longer pink, about 25 minutes.

Mandarin Orange Cake

This orange cake with creamy pineapple frosting is an unbeatable combination on its own, but it really shines when paired with a Golden or Blonde Ale.

1 (18.2 oz.) box yellow
    cake mix
3 eggs
¾ C. vegetable oil
1 (11 oz.) can mandarin
    oranges, undrained

1 (5.2 oz.) box instant
    vanilla pudding mix
1 (20 oz.) can crushed
    pineapple, undrained
1 (8 oz.) tub whipped
    topping

Preheat oven to 350°. In a medium bowl, combine cake mix, eggs, oil, and oranges with liquid. Transfer batter to two lightly greased 8″ or 9″ round layer pans or an angel food cake pan. Bake for 30 to 40 minutes, or until a toothpick inserted in cake comes out clean. Meanwhile, combine pudding mix and pineapple with liquid; mix well and let thicken for 10 minutes. Fold in whipped topping. Remove cake from oven and let cool before spreading frosting between layers and/or over top and sides of cake. Refrigerate until ready to serve.

Summer Ale

The overall impression of a Summer Ale is refreshing and thirst-quenching. It is light straw to golden in color with medium-low to medium bitterness and lasting malt sweetness. Late kettle additions, and perhaps even dry hopping, sometimes contribute to the forward flavor of hops, yet always balance with the malt character.

Summary Ale

Try it

Alaskan Summer Ale
Alaskan Brewing Company

Anchor Summer Beer
Anchor Brewing Company

Curve Ball
Pyramid Breweries, Inc.

Farmhouse Summer Ale
Flying Fish Brewing Company

Geary's Summer Ale
Geary's Brewing Company

Honey Moon Summer Ale
Blue Moon Brewing Company

Samuel Adams Summer Ale
The Boston Beer Company

Saranac Summer Ale
The Matt Brewing Company

Shiner Kölsch
The Spoetzl Brewery

Summer Ale
Fuller's Brewing

Summer Blonde
River Horse Brewing Company

Summer Lightning
Hop Back Brewery

Summerfest
Sierra Nevada Brewing Company

Summertime
Goose Island Beer Company

Sunrye Summer Ale
Redhook Ale Brewery

Serve at 40-45° F
Serve in Shaker Pint

Serve with

Summer Ale has a quenching zing of hop bitterness that should be enjoyed in the warm months, since most Summer Ales are seasonal brews lasting from May through August. Naturally, it is paired with many summer foods, such as barbequed meats, grilled fish, and summer salads.

Grilled Shrimp Skewers

A Summer Ale sets off this seafood dish with a spicy Latin influence. Serve over salad greens with a light vinaigrette dressing, or with tortilla chips and a fragrant tomato salsa.

3 cloves garlic, minced
⅓ C. extra-virgin olive oil
¼ C. tomato sauce
2 T. red wine vinegar
2 T. chopped fresh basil
½ tsp. salt

¼ tsp. cayenne pepper
2 lbs. fresh shrimp, peeled
  and deveined
Wooden skewers
Juice of ½ lime

In a large bowl, combine garlic, oil, tomato sauce, and vinegar; season with basil, salt, and cayenne pepper. Add shrimp to bowl and toss gently until evenly coated. Cover and refrigerate for 30 to 60 minutes, stirring occasionally. Soak wooden skewers in a bowl of water while shrimp is marinating. Preheat an outdoor grill to medium heat and lightly oil the grate. Thread shrimp onto skewers, piercing once near tail and once near head. Discard marinade. Cook shrimp for 2 to 3 minutes per side, or until they turn opaque. Remove shrimp skewers to a platter and lightly squeeze lime juice over top.

———————————————●———————————————

Fire-Grilled Garden Sandwich

Combine summer's best: grilled flavor and fresh garden vegetables. Can't you just feel the warm breeze?

¼ C. mayonnaise
3 cloves garlic, minced
1 T. lemon juice
1 C. seeded and sliced red
  bell peppers
1 small zucchini, sliced
1 red onion, sliced

1 small yellow squash, sliced
2 T. extra-virgin olive oil
2 (4″ x 6″) pieces focaccia
  or ciabatta bread, split
  horizontally
½ C. crumbled feta cheese

In a small bowl, combine mayonnaise, garlic, and lemon juice; cover and refrigerate. Preheat an outdoor grill to high heat and lightly oil the grate. Brush vegetables with oil on both sides. Place pepper and zucchini slices over hottest part of grill; surround with onion and squash pieces. Grill for about 3 minutes on each side, though peppers may take a little longer. Remove vegetables from grill and set aside. Spread some of the mayonnaise mixture over the cut side of each slice of bread and sprinkle with feta cheese. Place on grill, cheese side up; cover grill and heat for 2 to 3 minutes. Remove from grill and layer vegetables over each bread slice. Serve as open-faced sandwiches.

Honey Chicken
with Summer Salad

This recipe highlights the bounty of summer and is the perfect match for a refreshing Summer Ale.

1 (15 oz.) can red kidney
   beans, drained and rinsed
1 C. fresh corn kernels
1 small onion, diced
1 C. halved cherry tomatoes
2 T. lime juice
1 T. extra-virgin olive oil
Salt and pepper to taste

2 T. butter or margarine
1 clove garlic, minced
⅓ C. honey
1 T. lemon juice
4 skinless, boneless chicken
   breast halves
⅓ C. thinly sliced
   fresh basil

Preheat an outdoor grill to medium heat and lightly oil the grate. In a medium bowl, combine beans, corn, onion, tomatoes, and lime juice. Drizzle with oil and season with salt and pepper; toss until well mixed, then set aside. Melt butter in a small skillet over medium heat. Add garlic and sauté until fragrant. Whisk in honey and lemon juice. Set aside half of the sauce for basting. Brush remaining sauce over chicken. Grill chicken for 6 to 8 minutes on each side; turn and baste often with reserved sauce. Transfer chicken to serving plates and cover with a generous amount of Summer Salad. Sprinkle basil over each serving.

———————————•———————————

Fresh Peach Cobbler

This sweet summer dessert, along with a seasonal Summer Ale, is a great way to complete an alfresco lunch or dinner.

3 peaches, peeled, pitted
   and sliced
1 tsp. ground cinnamon
2½ C. sugar, divided
½ C. shortening

1 C. milk
1½ C. flour
2 tsp. baking powder
½ tsp. salt
3 T. butter

Preheat oven to 350°. In a medium bowl, combine peaches, cinnamon, and 1½ cups sugar; set aside. In a separate bowl, cream together shortening and remaining sugar. Alternately, add milk with flour, baking powder, and salt. Pour batter into a greased 8″ or 9″ square baking dish. Top with peach mixture. Drop butter into 2 cups boiling water; mix lightly and pour all over peaches. Bake for 40 to 45 minutes or until cobbler is golden brown.

Pilsener

German-style and American-style Pilsener is light straw to deep golden in color, while Bohemian-style Pilsener can be almost light amber in color. Pilsener has a moderate to high hop bitterness. The noble-type hop aroma and flavor are moderate yet obvious, and the head of a Pilsener is dense and rich.

Pilsener

Try it

Becks Pilsner
Brauerei Beck & Co KG

Greenshields Pilsner
Greenshields Brewery

König Pilsener
König Brauerei

Köstritzer Edel Pils
Köstritzer Schwarzbier Brauerei

Marquette Pilsner
Stone Cellar Brewpub

Moonlight Pils
Moonlight Brewing Company

Penn Pilsner
Pennsylvania Brewing Company

Pils Czech Style Pilsner
Lagunitas Brewing Company

Pilsner Urquell
Plzeňský Prazdroj

Polestar Pilsner
Left Hand Brewing Company

Portage Bay Pilsener
Maritime Pacific Brewing Company

Samuel Adams Boston Lager
The Boston Beer Company

Special Pilsner
Capital Brewery

Totally Naked
New Glarus Brewing Company

Zephyrus Pilsner
Elysian Brewing Company

Serve at 40-45° F
Serve in Footed Pilsner

Serve with

Pilsener can be a great accompaniment for lighter flavors
from the grill or broiler, such as chicken, salmon, or
bratwurst. It also makes a great thirst-quenching beer for
spicy Mexican, Thai, or Chinese dishes. Cream soups,
broccoli, and green salads with creamy dressings make
a good match. When it comes to cheese, serve Gouda,
Havarti, Muenster, young provolone, or buttery Vermont
White Cheddar with a Pilsener.

Shrimp & Crab Bisque

The hoppiness of a Pilsener complements this simple-to-make creamy seafood bisque.

2 T. butter
2 T. flour
½ tsp. salt
¼ tsp. white pepper
1 tsp. chicken bouillon
  granules
2 T. finely chopped onion
1½ C. half n' half, divided

½ lb. medium shrimp,
  peeled and deveined
½ lb. canned or lump
  crabmeat, drained and
  picked over
½ C. white wine

Melt butter in a medium soup pot over low heat. Stir in flour, salt, white pepper, bouillon, and onion. Blend in ¾ cup half n' half, then mix in shrimp and crabmeat. Increase temperature to medium and continue stirring until mixture thickens. Blend in wine and remaining half n' half. Continue to heat for 5 minutes. Ladle bisque into bowls and serve with chunks of crusty bread.

Chicken Enchiladas

Wash down this spicy Mexican dish with an American-style or German-style Pilsener.

2 T. extra-virgin olive oil
1 (4 oz.) can diced green
  chiles, drained
1 jalapeno pepper, seeded
  and chopped
1 clove garlic, minced
1 (8 oz.) pkg. cream cheese

2 C. shredded Monterey
  Jack cheese, divided
4 skinless, boneless chicken
  breast halves, cooked and
  shredded or chopped
8 (10″) flour tortillas
1 C. heavy cream

Preheat oven to 375°. Heat oil in a large skillet over medium heat. Add chiles, jalapeno, and garlic; sauté until fragrant. Stir in cream cheese and 1 cup shredded cheese. Gradually stir in ½ cup water as cheese begins to melt. Add chicken to skillet and mix well; remove from heat. Divide chicken mixture evenly onto tortillas. Roll each tortilla and place seam side down in a 9″ x 13″ baking dish. Sprinkle remaining cheese over top and pour cream over all. Bake for 30 minutes, or until enchiladas are golden brown on top.

Chicken & Broccoli Braid

The crispness of the broccoli, along with the mild bite of the provolone, makes you want to reach for a Pilsener.

2 C. chopped cooked
   chicken
1 C. chopped broccoli florets
¾ C. shredded or cubed
   provolone
¼ C. seeded and chopped
   green bell pepper
¼ C. seeded and chopped
   sweet red pepper

1 clove garlic, minced
1 tsp. dillweed
¼ tsp. salt
½ C. mayonnaise
2 (8 oz.) tubes refrigerated
   crescent rolls
1 egg white, lightly beaten
2 T. slivered almonds

Preheat oven to 375°. In a medium bowl, combine chicken, broccoli, provolone, peppers, garlic, dillweed, and salt. Add mayonnaise and mix until well combined. On an ungreased baking sheet, unroll both tubes of crescent dough; pinch seams and two pieces together to make one long 12″ x 15″ rectangle. Spoon chicken mixture down center of dough. Cut eight strips along either side of center, each about 3½″ long. Bring strips from both sides up and over filling to braid; pinch ends to seal. Brush egg white over dough and sprinkle with almonds. Bake for 15 to 20 minutes or until crust is golden.

German Bratwurst

A classic German dish, bratwurst makes a great accompaniment for a German-style Pilsener. Try boiling them in your favorite Pilsener beer!

6 fresh bratwurst sausages
1 onion, thinly sliced
½ C. butter
3 (12 oz.) cans or bottles
   Pilsener beer

¾ tsp. pepper
6 hoagie rolls

Prick bratwurst with a fork. Place them in a medium soup pot. Add onion, butter, beer, and pepper. Place pot over medium heat and bring to a simmer for 15 to 20 minutes; drain. Preheat an outdoor grill to medium-high heat and lightly oil the grate. Cook bratwurst on grill for 10 to 14 minutes, turning occasionally to brown evenly. Place some of the cooked onions on each hoagie roll. Place one cooked bratwurst over onions on each roll.

Egyptian stonecutters, slaves, and public officials were often paid for their labor with a type of beer called "kash", which may be a reason for the American derivative "cash".

Light Lager

Light Lager is very pale in color and body, and the hop flavor, aroma, and bitterness are insignificant to the taste. Light Lagers are generally highly carbonated. Low calorie versions do not exceed 125 per 12 ounces, while low carbohydrate versions have a maximum level of 3.0 grams per 12 ounces.

Light Lager

Try it

Abita Light
Abita Brewing Company

Bud Light
Anheuser-Busch

Coors Light
Coors Brewing Company

Heineken Premium Light Lager
Heineken International

IC Light
Iron City Brewing Company

Miller Lite
Miller Brewing Company

Molson Canadian Light
Molson USA

Mountain Light
Smoky Mountain Brewery

Old Milwaukee Light
Joseph Schlitz Brewing Company

Premier Light
Stevens Point Brewery

Sam Adams Light
The Boston Beer Company

Shiner Light
Spoetzl Brewery

Southpaw Light
Miller Brewing Company

Superior Light
Walkerville Brewing Company

Tecate Light
Cervecería Cuauhtémoc Moctezuma

Serve at 40-45° F
Serve in Footed Pilsner

Serve with

Many cuisines are finely paired with Light Lager, since the flavor and bitterness of this beer style is mild and very low. A common pairing is barbequed foods, as well as Latin American, Italian, Thai, Chinese, Japanese, Mediterranean, and Pan-Asian foods. Food spiced with curry makes a good match for Light Lager.

Hearts of Palm Salad

This is a Latin American dish, classically from the country of Costa Rica. A Light Lager won't overpower the natural flavors in the dish.

2 (16 oz.) cans hearts
  of palm
1 T. chopped fresh parsley
⅓ C. seeded and chopped
  red bell pepper
⅓ C. seeded and chopped
  yellow bell pepper

1 T. fresh lemon juice
1 T. Dijon mustard
2 T. low-sodium chicken
  broth
1 T. extra-virgin olive oil
Pepper to taste
Lettuce leaves

Drain hearts of palm and cut them into ½″ pieces. Place them in a medium bowl and add chopped parsley and peppers. In a small bowl, whisk together lemon juice, mustard, chicken broth, and oil. Season to taste with pepper and, if desired, add just a small amount of salt. Line a serving bowl with lettuce leaves and spoon salad into bowl.

———————————•———————————

Ginger Curried Chicken

This simple version of Thai curried chicken complements a Light Lager. Serve hot over a bed of white rice.

2 T. vegetable oil
4 skinless, boneless chicken
  breast halves, cut into
  1″ pieces
½ C. cornstarch
3 cloves garlic, crushed
1 large onion, coarsely
  chopped

Salt and pepper to taste
½ C. sherry wine
2 beef bouillon cubes
½ C. creamy peanut butter
3 T. curry powder
½ tsp. ground ginger
1 C. coconut milk

Heat oil in a large skillet over medium-high heat. Coat chicken pieces with cornstarch and add to skillet along with garlic, onion, salt, and pepper. Stir in sherry and bouillon. Heat, stirring occasionally, until liquid has reduced a little. Stir in peanut butter and curry powder. Add enough water to just cover the ingredients. Stir in ginger, reduce heat to low and let simmer for 30 minutes. Stir in coconut milk right before serving. Mix well and serve hot.

Greek-Style Penne

A Light Lager balances this Mediterranean pasta, seasoned with fresh tomatoes, feta cheese, and dill.

4 C. chopped, seeded fresh tomatoes
1 C. chopped green onions
7 oz. crumbled feta cheese
6 T. chopped fresh parsley
¼ C. chopped fresh dillweed
¼ C. extra-virgin olive oil
12 oz. uncooked penne pasta
Salt and pepper to taste

In a large bowl, toss together tomatoes, green onions, cheese, parsley, dillweed, and oil; set aside. Bring a large pot of lightly salted water to a boil. Add pasta and cook until tender but still firm, stirring occasionally; drain. Add hot pasta to tomato mixture and toss until well combined. Season lightly with salt and pepper.

Chicken Lettuce Wraps

Pan-Asian foods (combinations of flavors such as sweet and sour, jerk chicken and honey, Chipotle and lime, or gingered sesame and garlic) have just the right amount of spiciness and sweetness to be matched with a Light Lager. These lettuce wraps are a Pan-Asian favorite.

2 T. vegetable oil
2 skinless, boneless chicken breast halves, diced
¼ C. diced red onions
½ C. seeded and diced red bell pepper
¼ C. diced water chestnuts
½ C. diced mushrooms
¼ C. hoisin sauce
¼ C. sweet teriyaki sauce
3 T. chopped green onions
6 to 8 large iceberg lettuce leaves

Heat a large griddle or wok over high heat. Once surface is very hot, add oil and chicken; heat for 20 seconds then stir. Add onions and pepper; sear for 20 seconds. Stir in water chestnuts and mushrooms; sauté for 30 seconds. Add hoisin sauce and teriyaki sauce. Stir-fry ingredients for 1 minute or until steaming hot. Add green onions and toss well. Remove from heat and spoon mixture evenly onto lettuce leaves. Fold lettuce around filling and serve.

Lager

American-style Lager is light, clean, crisp, and highly carbonated. The flavor components are subtle with no one flavor or ingredient dominating the others. Vienna-style Lager, on the other hand, is reddish brown or copper in color. This beer style is characterized by light malt sweetness and a slightly toasted flavor, though hop bitterness is clean and crisp like American-style Lager.

Lager

Try it

Budweiser
Anheuser-Busch

Coors Original
Coors Brewing Company

Dos Equis
Cervecería Cuauhtémoc Moctezuma

Eliot Ness Amber Lager
Great Lakes Brewing Company

Foster's
Foster's Group Limited

Grain Belt Premium
August Schell Brewery

Leinenkugel's Original
Jacob Leinenkugel Brewing Company

Miller High Life
Miller Brewing Company

Narragansett
Narragansett Brewing Company

Old Style
G. Heileman Brewing Company

Red Stripe Jamaican Lager
Desnoes & Geddes Limited

Rolling Rock Extra Pale
Latrobe Brewing Company

Singha
Boon Rawd Brewery

Tsingtao
Tsingtao Brewery/Monarch Import Company

Tusker Premium Lager
East African Breweries Limited

Serve at 35-40° F
Serve in Lager Glass

Serve with

Traditionally, shellfish, barbequed foods, roast chicken, or sausages are served with Lager. More recently, the cuisines of Indian, Latin American, Thai, and Pan-Asian food have been matched with this beer style. Serve Lager with a peppery cheese, such as Pepper Jack.

Seafood Ceviche

This trio salad of citrus marinated seafood originated from Peru. Dish it into martini or margarita glasses and garnish with cilantro and lime for an elegant presentation. Serve with tortilla chips and your favorite Lager on the side.

½ lb. cleaned, cooked crawfish meat
½ lb. jumbo lump crabmeat, drained and picked over
½ lb. cooked small shrimp, peeled and deveined
½ C. lime juice
½ C. ketchup
2 T. hot pepper sauce
2 T. extra-virgin olive oil
⅓ C. chopped fresh cilantro
½ C. diced red onion
1 C. peeled, seeded, and diced cucumber
1 C. diced jicama
1 jalapeno pepper, seeded and minced
Salt to taste
1 large avocado, peeled, pitted, and diced

In a large bowl, combine crawfish, crabmeat, and shrimp. Pick any shells from meat and discard. Add lime juice to seafood; mix gently. Cover and refrigerate for 1 hour. In a small bowl, combine ketchup, hot pepper sauce, and oil. Stir in cilantro, red onion, cucumber, jicama, and jalapeno; add salt to taste. Gently fold ketchup mixture into seafood. Refrigerate until ready to serve. Fold in avocado just before serving.

Rosemary Roasted Chicken

Roasted chicken and Lager beer, especially the reddish-toned Vienna-style Lager, were made to go together.

1 (2 to 3 lb.) whole chicken, cut into pieces
½ C. butter or margarine
⅓ C. lemon juice
1 T. paprika
2 tsp. salt
1 tsp. pepper
1 tsp. brown sugar
½ tsp. dried rosemary
⅛ tsp. ground nutmeg
⅛ tsp. cayenne pepper

Preheat oven to 325°. Place chicken pieces in an ungreased 9″ x 13″ baking dish. In a small saucepan over medium-high heat, combine butter, lemon juice, paprika, salt, pepper, brown sugar, rosemary, nutmeg, and cayenne pepper; mix well and bring to a boil. Pour butter mixture over chicken. Bake, uncovered, for 90 minutes or until chicken juices run clear, basting occasionally.

Mulligatawny Soup

This is a variation of a traditional Anglo-Indian soup. The literal translation means "pepper water", though pepper is not a vital ingredient in the soup.

¼ C. butter
½ C. chopped onion
2 stalks celery, chopped
1 carrot, diced
1½ T. flour
1½ tsp. curry powder
4 C. chicken broth

½ apple, cored and chopped
¼ C. uncooked white rice
1 skinless, boneless chicken
　breast half, cubed
Salt and pepper to taste
Pinch of dried thyme
½ C. heavy cream, warmed

Melt butter in a large soup pot over medium-high heat. Add onion, celery, and carrot; sauté until tender. Stir in flour and curry powder; cook for 5 more minutes. Add chicken broth. Mix well and bring to a boil. Reduce heat to medium and simmer for 30 minutes. Add apple, rice, chicken, salt, pepper, and thyme. Continue to simmer for an additional 15 to 20 minutes, or until rice is tender. Just before serving, stir in cream. Ladle soup into bowls and serve.

Country-Style Pork Ribs

Barbequed ribs are the perfect thing to wash down with a cold Lager. The ribs can be boiled in water, but the flavor is even richer when a crisp Lager beer is used.

2½ lbs. pork spareribs
2 (18 oz.) bottles barbeque
　sauce
1 onion, quartered

1 tsp. salt
½ tsp. pepper
4 to 6 (12 oz.) bottles or
　cans Lager beer

Place spareribs in a large pot. Cover with barbeque sauce, onion, salt, and pepper. Add enough beer to cover ribs. Bring to a low boil over medium-low heat and cook for about 40 minutes. Preheat an outdoor grill to medium-high heat and lightly oil the grate. Remove ribs from pot and place on hot grill. Grill ribs for about 20 minutes or until nicely browned, turning and basting often with barbeque sauce from the pot.

Hefeweizen or Wheat Ale

HEFEWEIZEN

German-style Hefeweizen, along with American-style Wheat Ale, is pale to golden amber, and brewed with at least 50 percent malted wheat. It has a full body and high malty sweetness. German-style Hefeweizen usually has a lower alcohol content than the American-style Wheat Ale.

Hefeweizen • Wheat Ale

Try it

American Wheat
Upstream Brewing Company

Ayinger Bräu-Weisse
Brauerei Aying

Oberon Ale
Bell's Brewery, Inc.

Circus Boy
Magic Hat Brewing Company

DreamWeaver Wheat
Tröegs Brewing Company

Gumballhead
Three Floyds Brewing Company

Haystack Wheat
Left Hand Brewing Company

Hop Sun Summer Wheat Beer
Southern Tier Brewing Company

In-Heat Wheat Hefeweizen
Flying Dog Brewery

Paulaner Hefe-Weissbier Naturtrüb
Paulaner Brauerei München

Sierra Nevada Wheat Beer
Sierra Nevada Brewing Company

UFO Hefeweizen
Harpoon Brewery

Unfiltered Wheat Beer
Boulevard Brewing Company

Weihenstephaner Hefeweissbier
Brauerei Weihenstephan

Widmer Hefeweizen
Widmer Brothers Brewing Company

Serve at 40-45° F
Serve in Weizen Glass

Serve with

The clove accents of Hefeweizen and American-style Wheat Ale complement many salads, such as tangy potato salad or salads with vinegar-based dressings. Barbequed meats and fish also make a great match. Serve with simple chevre goat cheese, herbed spread, buffalo mozzarella, Wisconsin brick, or Edam cheese. Hefeweizen is easily overpowered by a sweet dessert, so choose something light with fresh berries.

California Roll

This sushi roll became well-known upon its invention in Los Angeles in the early 1970s. The California Roll has inspired sushi chefs to create non-traditional fusion cuisine, and is one of the major reasons for sushi's worldwide popularity. Pair this, and other maki-zushi or nigiri-zushi, with your favorite Hefeweizen.

3 T. rice vinegar
3 T. sugar
1½ tsp. salt
2 C. cooked sushi rice
4 nori seaweed sheets
½ cucumber, peeled and cut into small strips

2 T. pickled gingerroot
1 avocado, peeled, pitted, and finely cubed
½ lb. imitation crabmeat, flaked

Preheat oven to 300°. In a small bowl, combine vinegar, sugar, and salt. Blend this mixture into cooked rice; set aside. Place nori sheets on an ungreased baking sheet. Heat in oven for 1 to 2 minutes, or until warm and pliable. Center one nori sheet on a bamboo sushi mat. Wet your hands and use them to spread a thin layer of rice over the nori, pressing down lightly. Arrange ¼ of the cucumber, gingerroot, avocado, and crabmeat down center of rice. Lift end of mat and gently roll it over ingredients, pressing gently. Roll forward to make a complete roll. Repeat with remaining nori sheets and ingredients. Use a wet, sharp knife to cut each roll into four to six pieces.

———————————————●———————————————

Penne with Goat Cheese & Arugula

This fresh-from-the-garden pasta goes great with a Hefeweizen. The beer is light enough for the delicate flavors of the pasta and arugula, and the acidic carbonation will cut through the richness of the goat cheese.

2 C. uncooked penne pasta
5.5 oz. goat cheese
2 C. coarsely chopped arugula
1 C. quartered cherry tomatoes

¼ C. extra-virgin olive oil
2 tsp. minced garlic
½ tsp. salt
½ tsp. pepper

Bring a large pot of lightly salted water to a boil. Add pasta and cook until tender but still firm, stirring occasionally. Drain pasta and set aside. Meanwhile, crumble goat cheese into a large serving bowl. Add arugula, tomatoes, oil, garlic, salt, and pepper. Add pasta and toss everything together.

Tuscan Panzanella

This rustic Italian bread salad is usually served in the summer months. A refreshing Wheat Ale complements the flavors of balsamic vinegar, mozzarella, basil, and fresh tomatoes.

6 C. bite-size day-old Italian bread pieces
Salt and pepper to taste
3 cloves garlic, minced
⅓ C. plus ¼ C. extra-virgin olive oil, divided
2 T. balsamic vinegar
4 medium-ripe tomatoes, cut into wedges
¾ C. sliced red onion
10 basil leaves, shredded
½ C. pitted and halved green olives
1 C. bite-size fresh mozzarella cheese pieces

Preheat oven to 400°. In a large bowl, toss bread pieces with salt, pepper, garlic and ⅓ cup oil. Spread bread pieces on a baking sheet. Toast in oven until golden, about 5 to 10 minutes; remove from oven and set aside to cool slightly. In a small bowl, whisk together vinegar and remaining oil. In a serving bowl, gently toss together bread pieces, tomato wedges, onion, basil, olives, and cheese. Drizzle vinaigrette over salad. Toss lightly and let sit for about 20 minutes before serving.

German Potato Salad

This tangy version of potato salad has authentic German flavor, making it the perfect match for a German-style Hefeweizen.

12 medium red potatoes
1 medium onion, finely chopped
3 hard-cooked eggs, peeled and chopped
2 dill pickles, finely chopped
2 T. chopped fresh parsley
¾ C. chicken broth
¾ C. mayonnaise or salad dressing
1½ tsp. salt
½ tsp. pepper
¼ tsp. garlic powder
2 tomatoes, cubed
6 bacon strips, cooked and crumbled

Bring a large pot of lightly salted water to a boil. Add potatoes and cook until tender. Drain pot and let potatoes cool slightly. Peel and slice potatoes. In a large bowl, combine potatoes, onion, eggs, pickles, and parsley; set aside. Heat chicken broth in a small saucepan over medium heat until warm. Remove from heat and stir in mayonnaise, salt, pepper, and garlic powder; mix until smooth. Pour mayonnaise mixture over potatoes. Mix gently, then cover and chill in refrigerator until ready to serve. Just before serving, gently fold in tomatoes and bacon.

India Pale Ale

INDIA PALE ALE

English-style and American-style India Pale Ale (IPA) is characterized by medium to high hop bitterness with a medium to high alcohol content. It is brewed using water with a high mineral content, resulting in a crisp, dry beer. IPA ranges in color from pale gold to copper. IPA is the result of British brewers trying to make a beer that would keep well on long voyages in hot climates. The brewers used a higher alcohol content and hops to prevent the growth of bacteria that causes sourness in beer during long storage.

India Pale Ale

Try it

60 Minute IPA
Dogfish Head Craft Brewed Ales

AleSmith IPA
AleSmith Brewing Company

Avery IPA
Avery Brewing

Blind Pig IPA
Russian River Brewing Company

Centennial IPA
Founders Brewing Company

Full Sail IPA
Full Sail Brewing Company

Furious
Surly Brewing Company

Hop Ottin' IPA
Anderson Valley Brewing Company

Hop Rod Rye
Bear Republic Brewing Company

Inversion IPA
Deschutes Brewery

Liberty Ale
Anchor Brewing Company

Masala Mama India Pale Ale
Minneapolis Town Hall Brewery

Smuttynose IPA
Smuttynose Brewing Company

Stone IPA
Stone Brewing Company

Titan IPA
Great Divide Brewing Company

Serve at   50-55° F
Serve in   Shaker Pint

Serve with

IPA is the perfect beer to team up with spicy dishes.
Indian food is a natural pairing, as is Cajun, Thai, or
Mexican cuisine. But don't limit yourself to spicy foods.
IPA is also a great match for pork chops, pesto dishes,
or escargot. For cheese, pick a milder blue such as
Gorgonzola, Stilton, or Cambozola. Many bold, sweet
desserts, such as spice cake or rice pudding, can be
served with IPA.

Spicy Crab Cakes

These crab cakes are packed with flavor and spice, making them the perfect accompaniment for a hoppy IPA.

4 to 5 slices white
   bread, torn
¾ C. chopped fresh
   parsley, divided
1 large egg yolk
2 tsp. lemon juice
2 tsp. Worcestershire sauce
1½ tsp. hot pepper sauce
2 T. plus 1 tsp. Dijon
   mustard
½ tsp. paprika
½ tsp. dried thyme

½ tsp. celery seed
¼ tsp. pepper
5 T. extra-virgin olive oil
¼ C. chopped onion
¼ C. seeded and chopped
   green bell pepper
¼ C. seeded and chopped
   red bell pepper
1 lb. canned or lump
   crabmeat, drained and
   picked over
2 T. butter

Pulse bread pieces in a food processor until fine, soft crumbs form, about 4 cups. In a shallow dish, combine bread crumbs and ½ cup parsley. In a food processor, combine egg yolk, lemon juice, Worcestershire sauce, hot pepper sauce, mustard, paprika, thyme, celery seed, and pepper; pulse. While pulsing, add oil in a steady stream until mixture is consistency of mayonnaise; set aside. In a large bowl, combine onion, bell peppers, and remaining parsley. Add sauce and crabmeat; mix lightly. Fold 1 cup of the bread crumbs into mixture. Gently form 6 cakes, each about ½″ thick. Dredge cakes in remaining bread crumbs; cover and refrigerate for 1 hour. Heat butter in a large skillet. Gently fry cakes for 4 to 5 minutes on each side, or until golden brown and heated through.

Pork Chops
with Blue Cheese Sauce

Sip on your favorite IPA and taste this dish come to life! The hop bitterness will cut through the blue cheese and the crisp finish will encourage your next bite.

2 T. butter
4 thick-cut pork chops
½ tsp. pepper

½ tsp. garlic powder
1 C. whipping cream
2 oz. crumbled blue cheese

Melt butter in a large skillet over medium heat. Season pork chops with pepper and garlic powder on all sides. Fry pork chops in skillet, turning occasionally. Cook until pork chops are no longer pink, about 20 to 25 minutes; remove to a plate and keep warm. Pour whipping cream into same skillet over medium heat, stirring to loosen any bits. Add blue cheese and stir constantly until sauce thickens, about 5 minutes. Pour sauce over the warm pork chops.

Chicken Tortilla Soup

An IPA and this Mexican spiced soup make an incredible duo.

½ tsp. extra-virgin olive oil
2 skinless, boneless chicken
   breasts
½ tsp. minced garlic
¼ tsp. ground cumin
2 (14.5 oz.) cans chicken
   broth
1 C. frozen corn kernels

1 C. chopped onion
½ tsp. chili powder
1 T. lemon juice
1 C. thick and chunky salsa
1 C. small corn tortilla chips
½ C. shredded Monterey
   Jack cheese
Sour cream

Heat oil in a large pot over medium heat. Add chicken and sauté for 5 minutes. Stir in garlic and cumin. Add chicken broth, corn, onion, chili powder, lemon juice, and salsa. Reduce heat to low and simmer for 20 to 30 minutes. Remove chicken from pot and shred into small pieces. Return shredded chicken to pot. Ladle soup into bowls. Garnish each serving with a few corn tortilla chips, some cheese, and a dollop of sour cream.

Blackened Chicken

Everything from the grilled flavor down to the peppery white sauce in this favorite Cajun dish will stand out when paired with an IPA.

1 T. paprika
4 tsp. sugar, divided
1½ tsp. salt, divided
1 tsp. garlic powder
1 tsp. dried thyme
1 tsp. lemon pepper
   seasoning

1 tsp. cayenne pepper
1½ tsp. pepper, divided
4 skinless, boneless chicken
   breast halves
1⅓ C. mayonnaise
2 T. cider vinegar

Preheat an outdoor grill to medium-high heat and lightly oil the grate. In a small bowl, combine paprika, 1 teaspoon sugar, 1 teaspoon salt, garlic powder, thyme, lemon pepper seasoning, cayenne pepper, and 1 teaspoon pepper; mix well and sprinkle over all sides of the chicken; set aside. In a separate bowl, combine 2 tablespoons water, mayonnaise, vinegar, remaining sugar, salt, and pepper; mix well and set aside 1 cup in the refrigerator. Use remaining sauce for basting. Place chicken on grill over indirect heat; cover. Grill for 4 to 6 minutes on each side, basting frequently with sauce. Chicken is done when it is no longer pink and chicken juices run clear. Serve with reserved sauce.

Pale Ale

PREMIUM BEER

PALE ALE

English-style, American-style, and Belgian-style Pale Ale is golden to amber or copper in color. Hop bitterness is medium to high and should be evident in flavor and aroma. Earthy, herbal, floral, and citrus flavors are often perceived in the end tasting. Pale Ale is usually medium-bodied and low to medium in malt flavor.

Pale Ale

Try it

Alpha King Pale Ale
Three Floyds Brewing Company

Bass Imported Pale Ale
Bass Brewers Limited

Blue Heron Pale Ale
Mendocino Brewing Company

Devotion
The Lost Abbey / Port Brewing Company

Firestone Pale Ale
Firestone Walker Brewing Company

Harpoon Ale
Harpoon Brewery

Little Creatures Pale Ale
Little Creatures Brewing

London Pride
Fuller, Smith & Turner P.L.C.

Luciérnaga "The Firefly"
Jolly Pumpkin Artisan Ales

Monty Python's Holy Grail
Black Sheep Brewery

Old Brewery Pale Ale
Samuel Smith's Brewery

Red Seal Ale
North Coast Brewing Company

Sierra Nevada Pale Ale
Sierra Nevada Brewing Company

Stone Pale Ale
Stone Brewing Company

XP Pale Ale
Bear Republic Brewing Company

Serve at 50-55° F
Serve in English Pint

Serve with

Pale Ale lends itself well to a wide range of food. American-style and English-style Pale Ale is perfect with roast beef, prime rib, steak, burgers, and lamb dishes. It goes great with fried seafood, as well as rich-tasting poultry, such as goose, duck, or dark-meat turkey. Cheddar, Derby, and hard-aged cheeses complement this style, as well as warm pumpkin, maple, or banana-flavored desserts.

Lamb Chops
with Brown Sugar Glaze

Pair a Pale Ale with this dish to cut through and highlight the buttery richness of the lamb and sweetness of the outer glaze.

¼ C. brown sugar
2 tsp. ground ginger
2 tsp. dried tarragon
1 tsp. ground cinnamon

1 tsp. pepper
1 tsp. garlic powder
½ tsp. salt
4 lamb chops

In a medium bowl, combine brown sugar, ginger, tarragon, cinnamon, pepper, garlic powder, and salt. Rub lamb chops all over with seasonings and place on a plate; cover and refrigerate for 1 hour. Preheat an outdoor grill to high heat and lightly oil the grate. Arrange lamb chops on grill and cook for 5 minutes on each side, or to desired doneness.

Grilled Goose
with Prune Stuffing

This grilling method makes the goose moist and tender. Use Pale Ale in the stuffing and gravy to enhance the flavor of this multi-faceted brew.

1 (10 lb.) whole goose, rinsed, fat trimmed
2 tsp. salt
1 tsp. dried marjoram
8 oz. coarsely chopped prunes
1 C. Pale Ale, divided
2 C. peeled, cored, and chopped apples

1½ C. lightly packed, crumbled fresh rye bread
2 T. raisins
1 T. fresh lime juice
1 tsp. sugar
½ tsp. salt
¼ to ½ tsp. ground cinnamon

Preheat an outdoor grill to medium-high heat. Sprinkle salt and marjoram over inside and outside of goose. Prick skin all over with a fork. Place goose, breast side up, in a large roasting pan. Place pan on center of grate and add 2 cups water to pan. Cover and grill for 2½ to 3 hours, or until internal temperature reaches 180°F. Meanwhile, prepare stuffing by combining prunes and ¼ cup Pale Ale in a large bowl; soak for 5 minutes. Add apples, rye bread, raisins, lime juice, sugar, salt, and cinnamon; mix well. Place stuffing in a 4″ x 8″ aluminum pan. Cover with foil and grill over indirect heat for 40 minutes. To make gravy, in a medium saucepan over medium-high heat, mix remaining Pale Ale with ½ cup water, 3 tablespoons of the pan drippings from goose, and 3 tablespoons stuffing. Bring mixture to a boil, reduce heat and simmer for 5 minutes, stirring constantly. Strain gravy and season with salt to taste. Carve goose and serve with stuffing and gravy.

Cheddar, Onion, and Bacon Stuffed Burgers

An all-American favorite, this burger will bring forth every flavor in your Pale Ale of choice, and vice versa.

3 lbs. ground beef
¼ tsp. salt
½ tsp. pepper
3 T. barbeque sauce
½ tsp. garlic powder
½ lb. bacon, cut into
   ¼″ pieces

1 medium onion, finely
   chopped
¾ C. shredded Cheddar
   cheese
6 hamburger buns, split

In a large bowl, combine ground beef, salt, pepper, barbeque sauce, and garlic powder; mix by hand until well combined. Shape mixture into twelve patties. Place patties on a baking sheet, cover with plastic wrap, and refrigerate for 30 minutes. Cook bacon pieces in a skillet over medium-high heat until evenly browned. Transfer bacon to paper towels to drain, reserving drippings in skillet. Reduce heat to medium and sauté onions until soft and slightly browned. Combine onions and bacon in a small bowl. Preheat an outdoor grill to medium heat and lightly oil the grate. Remove burgers from refrigerator and top six patties with 1½ tablespoons each of the bacon mixture. Sprinkle cheese over same six patties; top with remaining six patties, pressing edges together to seal. Grill burgers until cooked through, about 3 to 4 minutes per side. Place each burger on a bun and serve.

Bananas Foster

Pair this dessert with an America-style Pale Ale with fruity and floral hop character.

¼ C. butter
⅔ C. dark brown sugar
3½ T. dark rum
1½ tsp. vanilla extract
½ tsp. ground cinnamon

3 bananas, peeled, sliced
   lengthwise and halved
¼ C. coarsely chopped
   walnuts
1 pint vanilla ice cream

Melt butter in a large skillet over medium heat. Stir in brown sugar, rum, vanilla, and cinnamon. When mixture begins to bubble, add bananas and walnuts. Cook 1 to 2 minutes, or until bananas are hot. Spoon ice cream into bowls; top with banana sauce.

Maibock & Heller Bock

German-style Maibock and Heller Bock are light straw to deep golden in color with a medium body and low hop bitterness. Maibock is often thought of as a pale version of Traditional Bock and, appropriately, the German word helle means light-colored. Some dispute that Maibock and Heller Bock are the same style, but they are generally agreed to be very similar. This style is often a seasonal beer brewed early in the year and tapped in the month of May.

Maibock • Heller Bock

Try it

Blonde Double Mai Bock
Stoudt's Brewing Company

Brinkley's Maibock
The Free State Brewing Company

Cuckoo Bock
Otter Creek Brewing

Dead Guy Ale
Rogue Ales

Fighting Finches Mai Bock
Tyranena Brewing Company

Heller Hound Maibock
Flying Dog Brewery

Hofbräu Maibock
Hofbräu München

JW Dundee's Pale Bock
Highfalls Brewing Company

Mai Bock
Sprecher Brewing Company

Maibock
Capital Brewery

Maibock
Summit Brewing Company

Maifest
August Schell Brewery

Penndemonium
Pennsylvania Brewing Company

Spring Bock
The Fort Collins Brewery

St. Boisterous Hellerbock
Victory Brewing Company

Serve at 45-50° F
Serve in Flute

Serve with

Perhaps surprisingly, Maibock is paired wonderfully with fried chicken. Other food matches include Thai or Korean barbeque. The high alcohol content of Maibock and Heller Bock make them a perfect beer for snack-type foods such as wheat crackers and Swiss Emmental cheese. For dessert, the warm honey notes of the beer complement rich desserts such as cheesecake or soufflé, as well as apple or walnut flavors.

Grandma's Fried Chicken

Though this dish may seem awfully greasy and overpowering, it is the perfect food to pair with a Maibock, whose hoppy crispness and spritzy carbonation make the flavors dance.

½ C. milk
1 egg, beaten
1 C. flour
2 tsp. garlic salt
1 tsp. paprika

1 tsp. pepper
¼ tsp. poultry seasoning
1 (4 lb.) whole chicken, cut
  into pieces
3 C. vegetable oil

In a medium bowl, whisk together milk and egg; set aside. In a large zippered plastic bag, combine flour, garlic salt, paprika, pepper, and poultry seasoning. Place chicken pieces in bag; seal and shake to coat. Remove chicken pieces and dip into milk and egg mixture. Return chicken pieces to bag and shake again to coat with flour mixture. Heat oil to 365°F in a large skillet over medium-high heat. Place coated chicken in hot oil, turning to brown all sides. Reduce heat to medium-low and continue cooking until chicken is tender and cooked through, about 30 minutes. Remove the chicken to paper towels to drain before serving.

Swiss Fondue

Swiss cheeses and a pale German Bock team up for a European adventure. Dip cubes of French bread between sips of your Maibock or Heller Bock.

1 C. dry white wine,
  Maibock, or
  Heller Bock beer
½ lb. shredded Swiss
  Emmental cheese
½ lb. shredded Swiss
  Gruyère cheese

2 T. flour
¼ tsp. salt
¼ tsp. nutmeg
1 (1 lb.) loaf French bread,
  cut into 1″ cubes

Bring liquid to a simmer in a fondue pot. Add the Emmental and Gruyère cheeses, ¼ pound at a time, stirring after each addition. Once cheese has melted, stir in next batch. Stir in flour with last batch of cheese. Once all cheese has been melted, stir in salt and nutmeg. Serve with French bread cubes for dipping. Other dippers could include: lightly steamed broccoli and cauliflower florets, button mushrooms, thick pretzel bites, toasted French bread cubes, cubed smoked ham, cooked hot sausage slices, or bacon-wrapped chicken skewers.

Korean Barbequed Steak

Choose a Heller Bock with a luxurious malt flavor and dry finish.
Together, this match will warm your soul.

½ C. soy sauce
5 T. sugar
2½ T. sesame seeds
2 T. sesame oil
3 shallots, thinly sliced
2 cloves garlic, crushed

5 T. mirin or Japanese
   sweet wine
2 lbs. thinly sliced chuck
   eye steaks
1 (8 oz.) bag cole slaw mix

In a large bowl, combine soy sauce, sugar, sesame seeds, oil, shallots, garlic, and mirin. Add thin steak slices, stirring until well coated. Cover and refrigerate for at least 12 hours. Heat a large skillet over medium heat. Once skillet is hot, add marinated steak slices and fry for 4 to 8 minutes or until steak is no longer pink. Fill six bowls with a portion of the coleslaw mix. Divide steak into six portions and place one portion over coleslaw in each bowl.

———————————————————•———————————————————

Walnut Apple Cake

The malty aroma and flavor of a Maibock or Heller Bock hints at
warm honey, making this cake a perfect match. Try to taste how the
beer brings forth each flavor in the cake.

1 C. sugar
1 C. vegetable oil
2 eggs
¾ C. honey
1 tsp. vanilla extract
2½ C. flour
1 tsp. baking powder

1 tsp. baking soda
1 tsp. salt
1 tsp. ground cinnamon
¼ tsp. ground allspice
3 apples, peeled, cored,
   and shredded
¾ C. chopped walnuts

Preheat oven to 325°. In a large bowl, combine sugar and oil. Beat in eggs until light, then stir in honey and vanilla. In a separate bowl, combine flour, baking powder, baking soda, salt, cinnamon, and allspice. Add dry mixture to egg mixture, stirring just until batter is moistened. Fold in apples and walnuts. Pour batter into a greased and lightly floured 9˝ Bundt pan. Bake for 50 to 60 minutes, or until a toothpick inserted in center of the cake comes out clean. Remove from oven and let cool for 10 to 15 minutes before inverting onto a plate and gently tapping pan to release cake.

Lambic &
Fruit Lambic

True Lambic is only brewed in the southwest Brussels area of Belgium. Versions of Lambic made outside of this area are called Lambic-style. Unblended Lambic is naturally and spontaneously fermented with an intensely sour and, sometimes, acetic flavor. This hazy beer is brewed with unmalted wheat and malted barley. Fruit Lambic is also sour, but characterized by strong fruit flavors and aromas.

Lambic • Fruit Lambic

Try it

Belle-Vue Kriek
Brasserie Belle-Vue

Boon Geuze
Brouwerij Boon

Bruocsella 1900 Grand Cru
Brasserie-Brouwerij Cantillon

Framboise
Brouwerij Lindemans

Geuze De Cam
Geuzestekerij De Cam

Gueuze 100% Lambic
Brasserie-Brouwerij Cantillon

Iris
Brasserie-Brouwerij Cantillon

Kriek
Brouwerij Lindemans

Kriek De Ranke
Brouwerij De Ranke

Lambik
Brouwerij 3 Fonteinen

Oud Geuze
Brouwerij Oud Beersel

Oude Kriek
Hanssens Artisanaal bvba

Rosé de Gambrinus
Brasserie-Brouwerij Cantillon

Saint Lamvinus
Brasserie-Brouwerij Cantillon

Samuel Adams Cranberry Lambic
The Boston Beer Company

Serve at 45-50° F
Serve in Stange

Serve with

Lambic is most appropriately served as an *apéritif*,
which is enjoyed as an appetizer before a large meal.
Therefore, many finger foods, tapas, fruits, and cheeses
are served alongside Lambic. Choose a sharp blue,
Limburger, Gorgonzola, or pungent Cheddar cheese.
On the other hand, Lambic can be served as a *digestif*,
which is consumed at the end of the meal, either alone
or with a fruit or small dessert course.

Pistachio &
Blue Cheese Grapes

A Fruit Lambic matched with this fruit and cheese combo performs magic as either an apéritif or digestif.

⅔ C. finely chopped
  pistachios
6 oz. crumbled Roquefort or
  Gorgonzola blue cheese

4 oz. cream cheese, softened
20 seedless red grapes

Preheat oven to 325°. Spread pistachios in an even layer on a baking sheet; toast in oven for 5 to 7 minutes. Remove pistachios from oven and set aside to cool. In a medium mixing bowl, cream together blue cheese and cream cheese until smooth. Spoon 1 tablespoon of the cheese mixture into the palm of one hand and roll the cheese mixture gently around one grape. Repeat with remaining cheese mixture and grapes. Place coated grapes on a baking sheet and chill in refrigerator for 15 minutes. Roll coated grapes in the pistachios until completely covered; return to the refrigerator to chill for 30 more minutes. Before serving, use a sharp knife to cut each grape in half.

———————————————•———————————————

Olive Tapenade
Stuffed Cherry Tomatoes

A dry, light-bodied Lambic coupled with a few of these beautifully-presented appetizers will wow any dinner guest.

½ C. Spanish olives with
  pimentos
1½ tsp. drained capers
1 tsp. brandy
¼ tsp. grated fresh
  lemon zest

2 T. extra-virgin olive oil
32 small cherry tomatoes
Chopped fresh parsley

Place olives in a food processor and pulse lightly to chop. Add capers, brandy, lemon zest, and oil; pulse until the ingredients are finely chopped. Using a sharp knife, slice the bottom ⅛″ off tomatoes so they will stand on a tray. Slice the top ¼″ off tomatoes and use a ¼ teaspoon to carefully scoop out juice and seeds, leaving shells intact. Spoon a generous ¼ teaspoon of the tapenade into each tomato shell; garnish with a sprinkling of parsley.

Spinach Tapas Tarts

Nothing will entice the palate more than these tarts paired with a Gueuze Lambic. It is the perfect combination to prepare diners for successive courses.

1 C. butter, softened
6 oz. cream cheese, softened
2 C. flour, sifted
1 (10 oz.) pkg. fresh or
   frozen spinach leaves
1 (19 oz.) can chick peas,
   drained and rinsed

1 red bell pepper, seeded
   and diced
1 T. minced fresh chives
Juice of 1 to 2 lemons
¼ C. extra-virgin olive oil
Salt and pepper to taste

In a medium bowl, blend together butter, cream cheese, and flour; refrigerate for 30 minutes. Preheat oven to 350°. Roll dough into small balls and press lightly into miniature muffin tins; bake for 5 minutes or until golden. Remove tarts from oven and let cool before removing from tins. Meanwhile, cook spinach. If using fresh spinach, steam over boiling water until leaves have wilted; drain, squeeze dry, and finely chop. If using frozen spinach, follow package directions to cook, then drain, squeeze dry, and finely chop. In a medium bowl, combine spinach, chick peas, pepper, chives, lemon juice, oil, salt, and pepper. Fill the cooled tart shells with spinach mixture and serve immediately.

Proscuitto Wrapped Shrimp

Try to note each flavor of this elegant appetizer while sipping on a Belgian Lambic. It's guaranteed to be a moment to savor.

12 large shrimp
Salt and pepper to taste
¾ C. crumbled Roquefort or
   Gorgonzola blue cheese
1 tsp. chopped fresh parsley
1 tsp. chopped fresh tarragon

1 tsp. chopped fresh chervil
1 tsp. chopped fresh oregano
2 tsp. minced garlic
12 thin slices proscuitto
2 T. extra-virgin olive oil

Peel and devein shrimp, leaving tails intact. Carefully butterfly each shrimp then season lightly with salt and pepper; set aside. In a medium bowl, combine blue cheese, parsley, tarragon, chervil, oregano, and garlic. Press about 1 tablespoon of the filling into cavity of each shrimp. Close and wrap one piece of proscuitto tightly around each stuffed shrimp. Heat oil in a large sauté pan over medium heat. When oil is hot, place stuffed shrimp in pan and sear for 2 to 3 minutes on each side, or until the shrimp turn pink and tails curl inward. Remove shrimp to a large plate and serve immediately.

Oktoberfest
& Märzen

Medium-bodied Oktoberfest, and similarly styled Märzen, is golden to reddish in color. In Germany, before refrigeration, it was nearly impossible to brew bottom-fermented beer in the hot summer. Therefore, many beers were brewed in March (Märzen), with the last beer brewed slightly stronger and stored until the autumn festivals. In general, American-style Oktoberfest has a greater degree of hop character than the classic German-style.

Oktoberfest • Märzen

Try it

Dogtoberfest
Flying Dog Brewery

Festbier
Victory Brewing Company

Hacker-Pschorr Original Oktoberfest
Hacker-Pschorr Bräu

Octoberfest Lager
Thomas Hooker Brewing Company

Oktober Fest
Stoudt's Brewing Company

Oktoberfest
Brooklyn Brewery

Oktoberfest
Millstream Brewing Company

Oktoberfest
Summit Brewing Company

Oktoberfest Lager
Berkshire Brewing Company Inc.

Oktoberfish
Flying Fish Brewing Company

Paulaner Oktoberfest-Märzen
Paulaner Brauerei

Samuel Adams Octoberfest
The Boston Beer Company

Saranac Octoberfest
The Matt Brewing Company

Spaten Oktoberfest
Spaten Muchen Bräu

The Kaiser Imperial Oktoberfest
Avery Brewing

Serve at 45-50° F
Serve in Dimpled Mug

Serve with

A classic German Lager, Oktoberfest is often paired with traditional German cuisine. In addition, Mexican food, sausage, pork, or any hearty, spicy dish complements this style. Oktoberfest is the perfect beer for a spicy jalapeno Jack cheese. For a dessert dish, almond biscotti, spiced cakes, and flan pair well.

Kraut Bierocks

The biscuit-like aroma of an Oktoberfest makes it the ideal beer to serve with bierocks, which are meat-filled pocket pastries originating from Eastern Europe. For a stronger kraut flavor, substitute sauerkraut for the shredded cabbage.

1½ (.25 oz.) pkgs. active
  dry yeast
½ C. sugar
4 C. flour
½ C. powdered milk
1½ tsp. baking powder
½ C. shortening
1 lb. lean ground beef
1 lb. ground Italian sausage

1 C. chopped onion
3 C. shredded cabbage
3 T. prepared mustard
2 tsp. salt
2 tsp. pepper
½ C. shredded processed
  American cheese
½ C. shredded Cheddar
  cheese

In a medium bowl, combine yeast, sugar, and 2 cups warm water; mix and let stand for 10 minutes. Stir in flour, powdered milk, baking powder, and shortening. Knead dough for 10 minutes, adding as little flour as necessary to keep from sticking. Cover bowl with a damp cloth and let rise in a warm place for 30 minutes, then knead again; set aside. To prepare filling, in a large skillet over medium-high heat, brown ground beef, Italian sausage, and onion; drain. Stir in cabbage, mustard, salt, and pepper; continue to heat for 5 minutes, stirring occasionally. Add cheeses; cook and stir until melted. Preheat oven to 350°. Flatten a 2 to 3 tablespoonful of dough. Place a large spoonful of filling onto dough and fold over to form a round bun, enclosing filling. Lay bun, seam side down, in a lightly greased 9″ x 13″ baking dish. Repeat with remaining dough and filling. Bake for 20 minutes, or until bierocks are golden brown.

The first Oktoberfest was actually the Munich wedding celebration of Crown Prince Ludwig and Princess Theressa of Bavaria on October 17, 1810. The party featured a horse race, beer, food, music, and dancing.

Celebrations continued each year in Munich. Almost a million people now show up for the annual Munich Oktoberfest, and consume some 750,000 spit-roasted chickens, more than 800,000 bratwursts and sausages, and almost 10 million pints of beer.

Today, Oktoberfests are celebrated from Japan to Canada, making it the second-most popular exported German custom (second only to the Christmas tree).

Jägerschnitzel

Enjoy a seasonal Oktoberfest with this delicious version of German schnitzel.

1 C. dry bread crumbs
1 T. flour
Salt and pepper to taste
1 egg, beaten
2 T. vegetable oil
4 pork steaks or cutlets, pounded thin

1 medium onion, diced
1 (8 oz.) can sliced mushrooms, drained
1 cube beef bouillon
1 T. cornstarch
½ C. sour cream

In a shallow dish, combine bread crumbs and flour; season with salt and pepper. Whisk egg in a separate dish. Dip steaks in egg and then into breadcrumb mixture, turning to coat all sides. Heat oil in a large skillet over medium-high heat. Fry steaks in oil for 5 minutes on each side or until browned. Remove steaks to a platter and keep warm. Add onion and mushrooms to skillet; sauté until lightly browned. Add 1½ cups water and bouillon, stirring until completely dissolved; simmer for 20 minutes. In a small bowl, combine cornstarch and sour cream. Stir sour cream mixture into skillet. Reduce heat to low and heat until thickened, being careful not to boil. Spoon mushroom sauce over steaks and serve immediately.

Pignoli Cookies

Pignoli, or pinoli, is the Italian word for pine nuts. Pignoli cookies, made of almond paste and topped with pine nuts, are an Italian specialty, and just the thing to equalize the faded bitterness in an Oktoberfest.

12 oz. almond paste
½ C. sugar
1 C. powdered sugar

4 egg whites, divided
1½ C. pine nuts

Preheat oven to 325°. Line two baking sheets with foil; spray with non-stick cooking spray. In a food processor, combine almond paste and sugar; process until smooth. Add powdered sugar and 2 egg whites; process until smooth. Whisk remaining egg whites in a small bowl and place pine nuts on a plate. With lightly floured hands, roll dough into 1″ balls. Coat balls in egg whites, shaking off any excess, then roll in pine nuts, pressing lightly. Arrange balls on the baking sheets and flatten to 1½″ rounds. Bake for 15 to 18 minutes or until just lightly browned. Remove from oven and place on wire racks to cool completely.

Amber Ale & Amber Lager

American-style Amber Ale and Amber Lager encompass a large category of beers that range from amber to reddish brown to copper in color. Amber Ale has a higher hop bitterness and flavor than Amber Lager. Both have a noticeable degree of caramel-type malt character, creating a characteristic malt-hop balance.

Amber Ale • Amber Lager

Try it

Amber Ale
Bell's Brewery, Inc.

Amber Waves Ale
Capitol City Brewing Company

Anniversary Ale
Amherst Brewing Company

Avalanche Ale
Breckenridge Brewery

CascaZilla
Ithaca Beer Company

Copperline Amber Ale
Carolina Brewery

Fat Tire Amber Ale
New Belgium Brewing Company

Iron Range Amber Lager
James Page Brewing Company

Nugget Nectar Ale
Tröegs Brewing Company

Red Rocket Ale
Bear Republic Brewing Company

Red Tail Ale
Mendocino Brewing Company

Santa's Private Reserve Ale
Rogue Ales

Steam Engine Lager
Steamworks Brewing Company

Stone Levitation Ale
Stone Brewing Company

Toasted Lager
Blue Point Brewing Company

Serve at 45-50° F
Serve in Shaker Pint

Serve with

Amber Ale and Lager have just the right blend of sweetness and spice, giving them the ability to stand up to garlicky pizza, a thick spicy burger, or a big bowl of chili. They match well with hearty dishes, including roast beef sandwiches, savory lamb stew, and many grilled meats. They join up equally well with Cheddar, Port-Salut, smoked, dry-aged, and tangy cheeses. For dessert, there is nothing more appropriate than poached pears. Bread pudding, banana, and pecan flavors also make great dessert choices.

Chili in Bread Bowls

Any spicy chili will go perfectly with an Amber beer. This recipe includes just the right amount of spice and is flavored with Amber Ale or Lager (or any dark beer). The easy-to-make bread bowls can be devoured as well!

1 (1 lb.) loaf frozen
  bread dough
2½ lbs. ground beef
3 stalks celery, diced
2 large onions, diced
2 cloves garlic, minced
3 T. extra-virgin olive oil
1 (29 oz.) can tomato sauce
1 (28 oz.) can crushed
  tomatoes, undrained
1 (6 oz.) can sliced
  mushrooms, drained

1½ C. Amber Ale or Lager
2 (16 oz.) cans chili
  beans, drained
1 (15 oz.) can kidney
  beans, drained
1 T. ground cumin
¼ C. chili powder
2 tsp. ground coriander
2 tsp. cayenne pepper
Dash of Worcestershire
  sauce

To make four bread bowls, thaw frozen dough in refrigerator overnight. Once thawed, cut dough into fourths; shape each section into a circular dome. Place domes on a baking sheet, cover, and let rise in a warm place for 4 to 7 hours. Preheat oven to 350°. Bake dough for 20 to 25 minutes or until golden brown. Let cool before cutting top ¼ off bread and scooping out some of the bread inside. To make chili, brown ground beef in a large skillet over medium heat; drain. In a large soup pot over medium heat, sauté celery, onions, and garlic in oil. Stir in cooked beef, tomato sauce, tomatoes with liquid, mushrooms, beer, chili beans, kidney beans, cumin, chili powder, coriander, cayenne, and Worcestershire sauce. Simmer, uncovered, over low heat for 3 hours. Ladle chili into prepared bread bowls.

O*ne theory for the common phrase "mind your P's and Q's" is as follows:*
In England, ale is ordered by pints and quarts. In old English pubs, when customers became unruly, the bartender would yell a warning for the patrons to settle down and mind their own P's and Q's (pints and quarts).

Garlic Chicken Pizza

Take a classic combination to the next level by pairing this gourmet pie with your Amber Ale or Lager of choice. Use refrigerated pizza dough or make your own.

2 T. cornmeal
1 (13.8 oz.) tube refrigerated pizza crust dough
1 C. Roasted Garlic Parmesan pasta sauce
¼ tsp. granulated garlic or ½ tsp. garlic salt
2½ C. shredded mozzarella cheese

2 skinless, boneless chicken breasts, grilled and diced
¼ red onion, sliced
1 tomato, cut into thin wedges
1 green bell pepper, seeded and diced

Preheat oven to 475°. Sprinkle a large pizza pan with cornmeal. Roll or pat dough out on a lightly floured surface until it covers the diameter of the pan. Place dough on pan; spread with pasta sauce and sprinkle with garlic salt and cheese. Arrange chicken, onion, tomato, and pepper over cheese. Bake for 20 to 25 minutes, or until dough is browned and cheese is melted.

———————————————•———————————————

Irish Lamb Stew

This Irish feast is hearty and delicious: the perfect meal to match up with an Amber Ale or Lager.

1½ lbs. thickly sliced bacon, diced
1 (6 lb.) boneless lamb shoulder, cut into 2″ pieces
½ tsp. salt
½ tsp. pepper
½ C. flour
3 cloves garlic, minced
3 large onions, chopped, divided

4 C. beef broth
2 tsp. sugar
4 C. diced carrots
3 potatoes, cubed
1 tsp. dried thyme
2 bay leaves
1 C. white wine

Fry bacon in a large skillet over medium-high heat until evenly browned. Transfer bacon to paper towels to drain; crumble and set aside. In a large bowl, toss together lamb meat, salt, pepper, and flour. Brown meat in bacon drippings in same skillet. Transfer meat to a large soup pot over medium heat. In same skillet, sauté garlic and 1 chopped onion until tender. Add ½ cup water, stirring to deglaze pan. Transfer liquid and garlic mixture to pot. Add bacon, beef broth, and sugar to pot; cover and simmer for 1½ hours. Stir in remaining onions, carrots, potatoes, thyme, bay leaves, and wine. Reduce heat to low and simmer for 20 minutes or until vegetables are tender. Discard bay leaves before serving.

Traditional Bock

Traditional German-style Bock is made with all malt, contributing to its complex toasty flavors. This bottom-fermented beer can range in color from light copper to dark brown with reddish highlights. Despite its dark color, Traditional Bock has good clarity, along with a low hop bitterness, allowing a slight sweetness to linger.

Traditional Bock

Try it

Aass Bock Beer
Aass Brewery

Anchor Bock Beer
Anchor Brewing Company

Berghoff Famous Bock Beer
Joseph Huber Brewery

Blonde Bock
Gordon Biersch Brewing Company

Caramel Bock
August Schell Brewery

KnuckleBall
Stone Coast Brewing Company

LTD Series No.1
Full Sail Brewing Company

Michelob Amber Bock
Anheuser-Busch

Rockefeller Bock
Great Lakes Brewing Company

Schokolade Bock
Millstream Brewing Company

Shiner Bock
The Spoetzl Brewery

St. Nikolaus Bock Bier
Pennsylvania Brewing Company

Uff-da Bock
New Glarus Brewing Company

Ur-Bock
Einbecker Brauhaus

Winter Brew
Sprecher Brewing Company

Serve at 45-50° F
Serve in Stein

Serve with

Just as other German-originating beers pair well with German cuisine, so does Traditional Bock. However, Bock beer also has the ability to wrap its concentrated malt flavor around food, making dishes such as wild game or dark meat blend right into the meal. Earthy cheeses, such as Camembert or fontina, make good matches. Custard or moderately sweetened chocolate are the most suitable choices for dessert.

Chicken Camembert

The thick and creamy Camembert sauce garners the spotlight in this recipe, and it is highlighted even more when coupled with a light copper Bock. Round out the meal with steamed fresh vegetables.

3 skinless, boneless chicken breast halves
2 T. butter
1½ T. flour
1 green onion, chopped
¾ C. milk

1 T. Dijon mustard
3 oz. Camembert cheese, cubed
1 avocado, peeled, pitted, and sliced

Spray a large skillet with non-stick cooking spray and place over medium heat. Once the skillet is hot, fry chicken breasts until browned on all sides and cooked through, about 20 minutes. Meanwhile, melt butter in a small skillet over medium heat; stir in flour until smooth. Add green onion and cook, stirring constantly, until mixture begins to brown. Gradually stir in milk; continue cooking and stirring until sauce is thick and smooth. Remove small skillet from heat and stir in mustard and Camembert cheese until melted and smooth. Place cooked chicken on serving plates and top each with several avocado slices. Pour cheese sauce over chicken and serve immediately.

Venison Backstrap

As the venison version of Filet Mignon, this recipe calls for the tenderest cut of a deer. The twice-marinated venison chunks wrapped in thick bacon, along with the moderate sweetness of a hickory-flavored barbeque sauce, meld into one out-of-this-world meal when paired with a Traditional Bock.

2 lbs. venison backstrap, cut into 2″ chunks
4 C. apple cider

2 (12 oz.) bottles hickory-flavored barbeque sauce
1½ lbs. thick bacon slices

Place venison chunks in a shallow baking dish and add enough apple cider to cover them completely. Cover and place in refrigerator for 2 hours to marinate. Remove venison from refrigerator and pat dry. Discard apple cider and return venison to dish. Pour barbeque sauce over chunks, cover, and refrigerate for an additional 2 to 3 hours. Preheat an outdoor grill, preferably a charcoal grill, to high heat and lightly oil the grate. Wrap each chunk of venison in a slice of bacon, securing with toothpicks. Place venison pieces on grill so they are not touching. Grill, turning occasionally, until bacon is slightly burnt, about 15 to 20 minutes. Take care when turning venison pieces, as bacon grease will cause the grill to kick up flames.

Caramel Flan

Savor the delectability of this creamy dessert with every bite. The caramel sugar sauce combined with the toasted caramel flavor of a Traditional Bock work wonders together.

¾ C. sugar
1 (8 oz.) pkg. cream cheese, softened
5 eggs
1 (14 oz.) can sweetened condensed milk

1 (12 to 14 oz.) can evaporated milk
1 tsp. vanilla extract

Preheat oven to 350°. Cook sugar in a small heavy saucepan over medium-low heat, stirring slowly until golden. Pour melted sugar into a 10″ round baking dish, tilting to coat bottom and sides; set aside. In a large mixing bowl, beat cream cheese at medium speed until smooth. Beat in eggs, one at a time, until well incorporated. Beat in condensed milk, evaporated milk, and vanilla until smooth; pour into pan over caramel coating. Line inside of a roasting pan with a damp kitchen towel. Carefully place round baking dish on towel inside roasting pan. Place roasting pan on oven rack and fill with boiling water to reach halfway up sides of filled baking dish. Bake for 50 to 60 minutes, or until center of flan is just set. Remove from oven and carefully remove flan dish from roasting pan. Let flan cool for 1 hour before transferring to refrigerator to chill for 8 hours or overnight. To unmold, run a knife around edge of pan and quickly invert flan and caramel sauce onto a rimmed serving platter. The flan can also be prepared in individual ramekins. If using ramekins, reduce baking time by 10 to 15 minutes.

In 1996, a British brewery made beer from a recipe taken from the walls of the tomb of Egyptian boy king Tutankhamun. Archaeologists examined tomb paintings, grains, and seeds left behind by ancient brewers, as well as beer sediment from excavated jars.

In reconstructing the recipe, the brewers used emmer, an ancient wheat grown by the Egyptians, and coriander, an herb found in the Nile region. The brewers collected enough raw materials to make 1,000 bottles of beer. The first bottle sold in England for $7,200 – the highest price ever paid for a bottle of beer.

Dark Lager

STAR BEER
Dark Lager

STAR BEER
Dark Lager

The malt aroma and flavor of American-style Dark Lager is low but notable. The color of this beer style ranges from deep copper to deep, dark brown. In comparison, European-style Dark, or Münchner Dunkel, has a more pronounced malt aroma, and is often described as bread-like, chocolate-like, or roasted. Non-malt adjuncts are often used, and hop bitterness is very low in a Dark Lager.

Dark Lager

Try it

Blackened Voodoo
Dixie Brewing Company

Brasal Bock
Brasal Brewery

Dunkel Rico
Stewart's Brewing Company

George Killian's Irish Red
Coors Brewing Company

Heineken Dark Lager
Heineken International

Henry Weinhard's Classic Dark
Blitz-Weinhard Brewing Company

Leinenkugel's Creamy Dark
Jacob Leinenkugel Brewing Company

Munich Dark
Capital Brewery

Munich Dunkel
Red Rock Brewing Company

Roadrunner Red Lager
Thunder Canyon Brewery

San Miguel Dark Lager
San Miguel Corporation

Sleeman Honey Brown Lager
Sleeman Breweries Ltd.

St. Pauli Girl Special Dark
St. Pauli Brauerei/Crown Imports LLC

Warsteiner Premium Dunkel
Warsteiner Brauerei

ZiegenBock Amber
Anheuser-Busch

Serve at 45-50° F
Serve in Dimpled Mug

Serve with

The best foods to serve with Dark Lager are spicy, hearty foods often found in Latin American or German cuisine. Roasted, barbequed, smoked, or grilled meats stand up nicely to this beer style. Serve Dark Lager with a washed-rind authentic Muenster cheese. For a sweeter pairing, choose fruit tarts with nuts, candied fruits, or sweet dense cakes.

Herb-Crusted Roast

The wait for this mouth-watering roast is well worth it. Watch as a fairly inexpensive cut of meat, when rubbed with seasonings, topped with a tangy horseradish sauce, and served with a Dark Lager, turns into a dinner fit for kings!

¼ C. dry bread crumbs
2 T. extra-virgin olive oil
1 clove garlic, minced
1 tsp. ground mustard
1 tsp. dried savory
1 tsp. pepper
½ tsp. dried rosemary

1 (3 lb.) boneless
  chuck eye roast
1 C. sour cream
3 T. prepared horseradish
1 tsp. lemon juice
¼ tsp. salt

Preheat oven to 325°. In a medium bowl, combine bread crumbs, oil, garlic, ground mustard, savory, pepper, and rosemary. Rub seasoning mixture all over roast. Place roast on a rack in a shallow roasting pan. Bake, uncovered, for 1½ to 2 hours or until meat is tender and reaches desired doneness on a meat thermometer (145°F for medium-rare, 160°F for medium, 170°F for well-done). Let roast stand for 10 minutes before carving. Meanwhile, in a medium bowl, combine sour cream, horseradish, lemon juice, and salt; mix well and serve on the side.

———————————————●———————————————

Brazilian Stew

This hearty stew boasts a meaty combination of tender pork and spicy chorizo sausage. Serve this Brazilian favorite with a Dark Lager to warm up a chilly winter evening.

2 T. vegetable oil, divided
1 tsp. minced garlic
1 large onion, chopped
1 (12 oz.) pork tenderloin,
  cut into ½" cubes
1 (19 oz.) can black beans,
  drained and rinsed, divided

1½ C. chicken broth
3 chorizo sausages, cut
  into ½" pieces
2 bay leaves
Salt and pepper to taste

Heat 1 tablespoon oil in a skillet over medium heat. Stir in garlic and onion; sauté until onion is softened. Transfer onion and garlic to a soup pot; set aside. Add remaining oil to same skillet over medium-high heat. Add pork and cook until well browned. Meanwhile, pour ¼ cup water and ¾ cup black beans into a blender; pulse until finely chopped but not entirely smooth. Mix bean puree, remaining whole black beans, chicken broth, sausage, and bay leaves into soup pot. Place pot over medium-high heat and add pork. Bring to a boil, then reduce heat to medium-low, cover, and let simmer for 30 minutes. Season stew with salt and pepper before serving.

Smoked Sausage Casserole

Serve this hearty dish to complement a Dark Lager. The mild, smooth Muenster cheese next to the spicy, smoked sausage makes for an interesting and appealing combination.

6 to 8 potatoes, peeled
  and cut into thick slices
1 lb. smoked sausage, cut
  into 1″ pieces

¼ C. milk
½ lb. Muenster cheese
  slices, rind removed

Preheat oven to 375°. Place the potatoes and sausage slices in a greased 2-quart baking dish; bake, uncovered, for 1½ hours. Carefully remove the baking dish from the oven. Stir in the milk and layer the cheese slices on top. Return the baking dish to the oven and bake for an additional 10 to 15 minutes, or until the potatoes are soft and the cheese is melted.

Pomegranate Tart

Tangy fruit and a Dark Lager may seem like an unlikely pairing, but this tart is just sharp enough to complement the mild malty notes and high carbonation in the beer.

2½ C. flour
1½ C. superfine sugar,
  divided
1 C. unsalted butter, softened
6 eggs, divided

1 pomegranate
1½ C. heavy cream
1 C. passion fruit puree
Coarsely chopped walnuts

To make the crust, combine flour and ¾ cup sugar in a bowl. Beat 1 egg into flour mixture; add butter and beat to form a dough; cover with plastic wrap and refrigerate for 1 hour. Preheat oven to 375°. On a lightly floured surface, roll out dough to a 9¼″ circle; set aside for 30 minutes. Line a 9″ tart dish with dough and bake for 30 minutes; remove from oven and let cool. Once cooled, brush the yolk of another egg over crust and bake for an additional 5 to 10 minutes. Remove crust and cool. Reduce oven temperature to 300°. To make filling, cut pomegranate in half; scrape out seeds into a large bowl, stirring to split seeds into pieces. Add cream, passion fruit puree, remaining eggs, and remaining sugar. Mix well and pour into cooled crust. Bake for 1 hour, or until filling has set. To serve, cut tart into wedges. Garnish each serving with a few chopped walnuts.

Brown Ale

American-style and English-style Brown Ale ranges in color from deep copper to brown. Often, roasted caramel-like, chocolate-like, or coffee-like malt flavors are notable in both flavor and aroma. American-style Brown Ale has an evident hop aroma while English-style has a dry to sweet maltiness with very little hop flavor or aroma.

Brown Ale

Try it

Bender
Surly Brewing Company

Best Brown Ale
Bell's Brewery, Inc.

Brooklyn Brown Ale
Brooklyn Brewery

Ellie's Brown Ale
Avery Brewing

Harpoon Munich Type Dark
Harpoon Brewery

HazelNut Brown Nectar
Rogue Ales

Hobgoblin Strong Dark Ale
Wychwood Brewery

Indian Brown Ale
Dogfish Head Craft Brewed Ales

Ipswich Dark Ale
Mercury Brewing Company

Moose Drool Brown Ale
Big Sky Brewing Company

Newcastle Brown Ale
The Newcastle Breweries Ltd.

Nut Brown Ale
Samuel Smith's Brewery

Riggwelter
Black Sheep Brewery

The Duck-Rabbit Brown Ale
The Duck-Rabbit Craft Brewery

Turbodog
Abita Brewing Company

Serve at 50-55° F
Serve in English Pint

Serve with

Brown Ale is very versatile when it comes to food pairings. The balanced maltiness goes well with everything from spicy stir-fry, curry, or sausage, to roasted chicken, venison, or smoked seafood. It also pairs well with beef soups and vinaigrette-topped salads. As far as cheese goes, try Roquefort, Stilton, Gouda, or a crumbly Cheshire. Brown Ale matches up with many sweeter, nutty dessert flavors, such as cheesecake or apple pie. Some say an after-dinner cigar is the perfect thing to complement a Brown Ale.

Asparagus Vinaigrette Salad

An ideal side for a meal of roasted chicken, steak, or roast beef, this salad will bring forth a hint of nuttiness in your Brown Ale.

1¼ lbs. fresh asparagus,
  cut into 2″ pieces
1 (4 oz.) jar diced pimientos,
  drained
⅓ C. sliced green onions
½ C. extra-virgin olive oil
¼ C. cider or white
  wine vinegar

1 tsp. Dijon mustard
1 tsp. Worcestershire sauce
½ tsp. dried basil
½ tsp. salt
¼ tsp. pepper
¼ tsp. dried thyme

Cook asparagus pieces in a small amount of water in a saucepan over medium heat for 5 minutes, or until tender but crisp. Rinse asparagus in cold water and drain well. Place asparagus in a medium bowl; add pimientos and green onions. In a small bowl, whisk together oil, vinegar, mustard, Worcestershire sauce, basil, salt, pepper, and thyme. Pour vinaigrette over asparagus mixture and toss until evenly coated. Cover salad and chill in refrigerator for at least 2 hours prior to serving.

Sirloin Steaks with Roquefort Sauce

Savor each bite as you cap off this meal with a roasted-malt Brown Ale.

2 T. butter
1 T. extra-virgin olive oil
4 (5 oz.) beef sirloin steaks
Salt and pepper to taste
2 T. brandy

1 C. heavy cream
3 oz. crumbled Roquefort
  cheese
Fresh parsley sprigs

Melt butter and heat oil in a large skillet over high heat. Season steaks with salt and pepper and quickly sear them on both sides in skillet. Reduce heat to medium and continue to cook steaks for 5 minutes on each side, or to desired doneness. Remove steaks from skillet and keep warm. Pour brandy into skillet and stir to loosen any bits. Stir in cream and bring liquid to a boil. Continue to cook, stirring constantly, until sauce is thick enough to coat the back of a spoon. Mix Roquefort cheese into sauce, stirring until completely melted. Spoon sauce over steaks and garnish with parsley.

Spicy Mongolian Beef

A Brown Ale is the perfect complement to this spicy stir-fry. Serve it over rice for a heartier meal.

¼ C. soy sauce
1 T. hoisin sauce
1 T. sesame oil
2 tsp. sugar
1 T. minced garlic
1 T. crushed red
  pepper flakes
1 lb. beef flank steak,
  thinly sliced
1 T. peanut oil
2 large green onions,
  thinly sliced

In a medium bowl, whisk together soy sauce, hoisin sauce, sesame oil, sugar, garlic, and red pepper flakes. Add steak slices and toss until evenly coated. Cover bowl and refrigerate for 1 hour to overnight. Heat peanut oil in a large wok or nonstick skillet over high heat. Add green onions and sauté for 10 seconds before stirring in beef. Discard any remaining marinade. Cook, stirring constantly, until beef is no longer pink and begins to brown, about 5 minutes.

Maple Pumpkin Cheesecake

Save this pairing for a cool autumn day when the roasted maple flavors of the dessert and beer are at their prime!

1¼ C. graham cracker
  crumbs
¼ C. sugar
¼ C. butter, melted
3 (8 oz.) pkgs. cream cheese,
  softened
1 (14 oz.) can sweetened
  condensed milk
1 (15 oz.) can solid pack
  pumpkin
3 eggs, lightly beaten
1½ tsp. ground cinnamon
1 tsp. ground nutmeg
¾ C. maple syrup, divided
4 tsp. cornstarch
2 T. butter
½ C. raisins
½ C. coarsely chopped
  walnuts

Preheat oven to 325°. In a small bowl, combine crumbs and sugar; stir in butter. Press crumbs into bottom of a greased 9″ springform pan; set aside. In a large bowl, beat cream cheese and condensed milk until smooth. Beat in pumpkin. Add eggs and beat just until combined. Fold in cinnamon, nutmeg and ¼ cup syrup; pour over crust. Place pan on a baking sheet. Bake for 70 to 75 minutes or until center is almost set; place on a wire rack to cool for 10 minutes. Carefully run a knife around edge of pan; cool for 1 hour. Meanwhile, combine cornstarch and 2 tablespoons water in a small bowl. Melt 2 tablespoons butter in a saucepan over medium-high heat. Stir in remaining syrup and cornstarch mixture. Bring to a boil, stirring until thickened. Remove from heat and stir in raisins and walnuts. Cool sauce to lukewarm before spooning over cheesecake; refrigerate overnight, then remove sides of pan.

Barley Wine Ale

BARLEY WINE

BARLEY WINE
STYLE ALE

Despite its name, Barley Wine Ale is actually a beer and not a wine. However, it is one of the strongest beer styles with a very high alcohol content. Barley Wine Ale ranges in color from tawny copper to dark brown, has a full body, and long-lasting malty sweetness. The complexity of alcohol and fruity character is high but counterbalanced by a low to medium bitterness. Caramel and sherry-like flavors can be noted in this beer style.

Barley Wine Ale

Try it

Bigfoot Barleywine Style Ale
Sierra Nevada Brewing Company

Blithering Idiot
Weyerbacher Brewing Company

Druid Fluid
Middle Ages Brewing Company

Fred
Hair of the Dog Brewing Company

Heavy Seas Below Decks
Clipper City Brewing Company

Horn Dog Barley Wine
Flying Dog Brewery

Millennium Ale
Old Dominion Brewing Company

Monster Ale
Brooklyn Brewery

Old Horizontal
Victory Brewing Company

Old Marley Barleywine
Thomas Hooker Brewing Company

Old Numbskull
AleSmith Brewing Company

Old Ruffian Barley Wine
Great Divide Brewing Company

Olde School Barleywine
Dogfish Head Craft Brewed Ales

Ridge Runner
Rock Art Brewery

Vintage Harvest Ale
J.W. Lees & Co. Ltd.

Serve at 50-55° F
Serve in Snifter

Serve with

Barley Wine Ale is a dark, rich beer meant to be sipped and savored, preferably on a cold winter night in front of a roaring log fire. This beer style easily overpowers most main dishes, so reserve it for strong cheeses or desserts. Stilton cheese and walnuts is a classic pairing. For a dessert pairing, choose rich, sweet desserts with hazelnut, toffee, or chocolate flavors.

Stilton Spread with Red Pears

These decadent crackers are just the thing to snack on while sipping a Barley Wine Ale. Thin apple slices or yellow pear slices can be used in place of the red pear.

2 oz. chopped walnuts
8 oz. Stilton blue cheese
6 T. whipping cream

1 ripe red pear, thinly sliced
24 water crackers

Preheat oven to 350°. Spread walnuts in an even layer on a baking sheet; bake for 8 to 10 minutes, or until lightly toasted. In a medium bowl, gently blend together blue cheese and whipping cream until smooth. Stir in toasted walnuts. Chill spread in refrigerator until ready to serve. Spread about 2 teaspoons of the cheese spread over each cracker. Top each prepared cracker with two very thin slices of red pear.

Caramel Roll Brownies

These fancy yet easy-to-make brownies can hold their own against a strong Barley Wine Ale. No one has to know they came from a chocolate cake mix and packaged candies.

35 chocolate-covered
   caramel candies, such
   as Rolo
1 (18.25 oz.) pkg. chocolate
   cake mix

½ C. butter, melted
⅓ C. milk
2 eggs
1 C. dark chocolate chips
1 C. toffee baking bits

Preheat oven to 350°. Unwrap chocolate caramel candies; set aside. In a large bowl, combine cake mix, butter, milk, and eggs; stir until well blended. Press half of the thick batter into bottom of a greased 9″ x 13″ baking dish. Bake for 6 minutes. Remove from oven and sprinkle chocolate chips and toffee bits over layer in pan. Press caramel candies lightly into surface, in rows of 5 x 7 candies. Spread remaining batter over top. Return filled pan to oven for an additional 20 to 25 minutes, or until a toothpick inserted in center comes out clean. Let brownies cool before cutting into 35 squares.

Creamy Dark Chocolate Cake

For the utmost indulgence, pamper yourself with a piece of this chocolate cake while sipping on a Barley Wine Ale. Chocolate is the perfect pairing for the malty sweetness of this beer style.

3 C. flour
2½ C. sugar, divided
½ C. unsweetened cocoa
  powder
2 tsp. baking soda
½ tsp. salt
1 T. instant coffee powder
⅔ C. vegetable oil

2 T. white vinegar
2½ tsp. vanilla extract,
  divided
3 eggs, divided
1 (8 oz.) pkg. cream cheese
1 C. semi-sweet chocolate
  chips
1 C. finely chopped walnuts

Preheat oven to 350°. In a large bowl, combine flour, 2 cups sugar, cocoa powder, baking soda, and salt. In a small bowl, combine 2 cups hot water and coffee powder; mix into dry ingredients. Stir in oil, vinegar, 2 teaspoons vanilla, and 2 eggs. Mix batter until smooth and blended. Spread batter evenly into a greased and floured 9˝ x 13˝ baking dish; sprinkle with ¼ cup sugar. Bake for 45 to 60 minutes, or until a toothpick inserted in cake comes out clean. Meanwhile, in a medium mixing bowl, beat cream cheese with remaining sugar, vanilla, and egg; mix until smooth, then fold in chocolate chips and walnuts. Once cake has cooled, spread frosting over top and cut into squares.

Hazelnut Candy Crunch

Rich and sweet enough to stand up to a dark Barley Wine Ale.

1½ C. milk chocolate chips
½ C. sugar
½ C. butter

1½ C. chopped hazelnuts
2 T. light corn syrup

Line the bottom and sides of a 9˝ square baking dish with foil, extending foil a little past the edges of the pan; grease foil. Melt chocolate chips in a double boiler over boiling water. Quickly spread melted chocolate over bottom of prepared pan; refrigerate until hardened. In a small saucepan over medium heat, combine sugar, butter, hazelnuts, and corn syrup. Bring to a boil, mixing until well blended. Continue to heat until mixture reaches 250° to 265°F on a candy thermometer. Pour melted mixture over cooled chocolate, spreading to form an even layer. Refrigerate until hardened and cooled. To serve, break candy into pieces; store in an airtight container.

Scotch Ale or Wee Heavy

Scotch Ale, also known as Wee Heavy, is overwhelmingly malty and full-bodied, while hop flavor, aroma, and bitterness are very low. Scotch Ale, essentially a very strong Pale Ale, ranges in color from deep copper to brown. American-style Wee Heavy tends to have a higher Alcohol by Volume than Scottish-brewed Wee Heavy. The clean alcohol flavor and aroma in this beer style helps balance the dominant sweet maltiness.

Scotch Ale • Wee Heavy

Try it

Allagash Musette
Allagash Brewing Company

Arcadia Ales Scotch Ale
Arcadia Brewing Company

Dirty Bastard
Founders Brewing Company

Jinx
Magic Hat Brewing Company

Kilt Lifter
Moylan's Brewery

Kilt Tilter
Middle Ages Brewing Company

McEwan's Scotch Ale
Scottish Courage

Old Jock Ale
Broughton Ales Ltd.

Samuel Adams Scotch Ale
The Boston Beer Company

Scotch Silly
Brasserie de Silly

Scotch Style Kilt Lifter
The Pike Brewing Company

Skullsplitter
Orkney Brewery

Tasgall Ale
Highland Brewing Company

Traquair House Ale
Traquair House Brewery Ltd.

Wee Heavy
AleSmith Brewing Company

Serve at 50-55° F
Serve in Thistle

Serve with

Pair a Scotch Ale with grilled or roasted beef, lamb, wild game, or smoked salmon, as well as hearty soups and stews. Couple aged sheep or goat milk cheeses, such as Mizithra or smoky Idiazábal cheese, with Scotch Ale. As for dessert, choose chocolate or toffee shortbread, puddings, or rich cakes.

Mexican Eggs

Appropriate for lunch or dinner, this spicy dish works in harmony with the low smoke character present in many Scotch Ales.

¼ C. extra-virgin olive oil
20 mixed Piquillo and
  Anaheim chiles, seeded
  and cut into 2″ pieces
1 medium red onion,
  thinly sliced
2 cloves garlic, minced

1 (12 oz.) pkg. bacon,
  cut into 1″ pieces
4 plum tomatoes, chopped
6 eggs
4 (1″ thick) baguette slices
4 Idiazábal cheese slices
4 proscuitto or Jamón
  serrano ham slices

Preheat oven to 425°. Heat oil in a large oven-safe skillet over medium-high heat. Add peppers, onion, garlic, and bacon; sauté until softened, about 12 minutes. Add tomatoes and heat for 2 minutes. Beat eggs and add to skillet. Stir once to distribute peppers. Reduce heat to medium-low and cook slowly for 2 to 3 minutes. Place skillet in oven for 2 minutes. Top each baguette with 1 cheese slice; place in oven to melt cheese. Remove skillet from oven and cut eggs into four servings. Place 1 slice of proscuitto on each plate and top with 1 serving of eggs. Serve baguette slices on the side.

———————————●———————————

Roast Leg of Lamb

For a perfectly-done medium-rare, remove the roast from the oven when it reaches an internal temperature of 140°F, since the roast will continue to cook to 145°F.

½ C. orange juice
1 C. white wine
3 cloves garlic, minced
1 tsp. dried thyme
1 T. dried rosemary

¼ tsp. pepper
2 T. extra-virgin olive oil
1 (6 lb.) boneless leg of
  lamb, tied up
Salt and pepper to taste

In a blender, mix orange juice, wine, garlic, thyme, rosemary, ¼ teaspoon pepper, and oil. Place lamb and marinade into a large plastic zippered bag. Wrap again in another plastic bag; place in refrigerator for several hours or ovenight. Remove from refrigerator 30 minutes prior to roasting. Preheat oven to 425°. Place one oven rack in middle position. Place a pan on bottom rack to catch drippings. Remove lamb from marinade and pat dry; season generously with salt and pepper, place directly on middle rack, then roast for 20 minutes. Reduce oven to 325° and roast for an additional hour, or for 10 minutes per pound. Check internal temperature with a meat thermometer. Once roast reaches 140° to 160°F, remove it from the oven. Let roast sit for 10 minutes before cutting away string and slicing. Spoon drippings over roast, or use them to make a gravy.

Sticky Toffee Pudding

Combine two of the best creations from the British Isles: Sticky Toffee Pudding and Scotch Ale.

8 oz. dates, finely chopped
¾ C. unsalted butter,
   softened, divided
1 C. light brown sugar
4 large eggs
1¾ C. self-rising flour

2 T. instant coffee granules
1 tsp. baking soda
2 C. whipping cream
1 C. dark brown sugar
Powdered sugar
Real whipped cream

Preheat oven to 350°. Grease a 9″ springform pan with butter. Line bottom of pan with buttered parchment paper. Place dates in a small bowl with 1 cup boiling water; let cool for 1 hour. Beat together ½ cup butter and brown sugar in a large bowl. Add 2 eggs, one at a time, beating well after each addition. Add half of the flour and beat until blended. Add remaining eggs and flour, beating well after each addition. In a small bowl, combine coffee granules and baking soda; pour into date mixture, stirring until dissolved. Add date mixture to batter and beat until blended. Pour batter into prepared pan; set on a jellyroll pan and bake for 1 hour. To prepare caramel sauce, bring whipping cream, dark brown sugar, and remaining butter to a boil in a medium saucepan over medium-high heat. Reduce heat to medium-low and simmer for about 15 minutes, stirring often, or until sauce has reduced to about 1¾ cups. When pudding is done, remove it from oven. Let cool slightly, remove pan sides, then sprinkle powdered sugar over pudding. Cut into wedges and serve with a generous spoonful of caramel sauce and whipped cream.

Scotland has nurtured a unique brewing culture for much of its history. During the eighteenth and nineteenth centuries, Scottish brewers were very active in exporting beer around the globe. Despite the variety of beers produced in Scotland over the last few centuries, one particular flavor profile emerged: barley.

Barley produced in the north of Scotland most often becomes Scotch whiskey, while that grown in the south is better suited for making beer. In addition, hops refused to flourish in Scotland so Scots chose to brew with other bittering substances, such as ginger, pepper, and herbs.

Doppelbock

German-style Doppelbock is a full-bodied beer ranging in color from deep amber to dark brown. Malt sweetness is dominant, but similar to lightly toasted malt rather than caramel or toffee flavors. Alcohol by Volume is high with noticeable strength, ranging from 6% to more than 10%. Historic versions of this beer style were considered "liquid bread" by the Bavarian monks who first brewed Doppelbock.

Doppelbock

Try it

Andygator
Abita Brewing Company

Autumnal Fire
Capital Brewery

Butt Head Doppelbock
Tommyknocker Brewery

Celebrator Doppelbock
Brauerei Ayinger

Consecrator Doppelbock Beer
Bell's Brewery, Inc.

Korbinian
Brauerei Weihenstephan

Liberator Doppelbock
Thomas Hooker Brewing Company

Maximator
Augustiner-Bräu München

Optimator
Spaten Muchen Bräu

Salvator
Paulaner Brauerei

Samichlaus Bier
Schloss Eggenberg

Samuel Adams Double Bock
The Boston Beer Company

St. Victorious Doppelbock
Victory Brewing Company

Tröegenator Double Bock
Tröegs Brewing Company

Weltenburger Monastery Asam Bock
Klosterbrauerei Weltenburger

Serve at 45-50° F
Serve in Stein

Serve with

Rich, roasted foods, such as duck and pork, are good
matches for a strong Doppelbock. In addition, many
smoke- or salt-cured meats are often paired with this
beer style to offset its sweet maltiness. The classic cheese
pairing is Limburger, while German Chocolate Cake,
Black Forest Cake, and Rumtopf are traditional desserts
best served with a Doppelbock.

Limburger Sandwich

The only way to eat this famous sandwich is to wash it down with a German Doppelbock. If desired, slices of braunschweiger or sardines can be added. To contain the strong odor of Limburger, rinse or cut off the rind and store the cheese in a glass jar.

Brown mustard
Mayonnaise
2 slices rye bread or
   pumpernickel

2 slices Limburger
2 thick slices sweet onion

To make one sandwich, spread brown mustard on one slice of bread and mayonnaise on the other. Layer slices of Limburger and onion onto bread to form a sandwich.

Roast Duck

This stuffed duck recipe is rich and flavorful, making it a desirable companion for a Doppelbock.

1 (4 lb.) whole duck
Salt and pepper to taste
1 tsp. poultry seasoning
1½ tsp. butter
3 T. chopped onion

5 stalks celery, chopped
3 C. peeled, cored, and
   chopped apples
3 C. crumbled cornbread
1 T. extra-virgin olive oil

Rinse duck and pat dry with paper towels; rub all over with salt, pepper, and poultry seasoning. Melt butter in a small skillet over medium heat. Add onion and celery; sauté until tender. In a medium bowl, combine apples and cornbread crumbs; add sautéed mixture and toss together, adding a little water if necessary. Preheat oven to 350°. Fill duck with stuffing and sew shut with kitchen twine. Rub outside of duck lightly with oil. Place duck in a 9″ x 13″ baking dish. Bake for 60 to 80 minutes, or until internal temperature reaches 180°F.

The familiar Bass beer symbol, a red triangle, was registered in 1876. It is the world's oldest trademark.

Braised Pork Shanks with Prosciutto & Mushrooms

A rich and flavorful recipe like this calls for a beer that can hold its own, such as malty German Doppelbock.

1 oz. dried porcini mushrooms
Salt and pepper to taste
4 (1½ lbs. each) whole pork shanks with rind
4 T. extra-virgin olive oil, divided
1 large onion, chopped
1 C. chopped carrots
1 C. chopped leek

½ C. chopped celery
2 oz. prosciutto, chopped
6 cloves garlic, chopped
1 C. dry white wine
1 C. chicken broth
3 tsp. chopped fresh sage, divided
2 tsp. chopped fresh rosemary, divided

Combine mushrooms and 1 cup boiling water in a bowl; let stand for 30 minutes. Drain and chop mushrooms, reserving liquid. Preheat oven to 325°. Sprinkle salt and pepper over pork. Heat 3 tablespoons oil in a large oven-safe pot over medium-high heat. Add pork in batches and sauté until browned on all sides. Transfer pork to a jellyroll pan. Discard all but 2 tablespoons of the drippings from the pot. Reduce heat to medium and add onion, carrots, leek, celery, and prosciutto; cover and cook for 10 minutes, or until vegetables soften. Mix in garlic, wine, and mushrooms; bring to a boil, stirring up any bits stuck to the bottom. Add chicken broth, 1 teaspoon sage, 1 teaspoon rosemary, and reserved mushroom liquid. Return pork to pot, adding any liquid from pan. Arrange pork in a single layer and bring liquid to a boil. Cover pot and place in oven; bake for 1½ hours, turning every 30 minutes. Increase temperature to 425°. Transfer pork back to jellyroll pan; brush with remaining oil, and sprinkle with remaining sage, rosemary, and pepper. Roast pork, uncovered, until browned, about 20 minutes. Meanwhile, skim any fat from surface of liquid in pot. Bring liquid to a boil until it is thick enough to coat the back of a spoon, about 7 minutes; season with salt and pepper. Divide vegetables and sauce into four shallow bowls. Top each with one pork shank.

Rauchbier

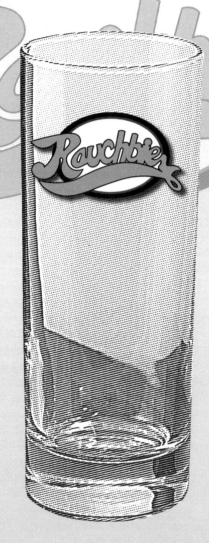

Bamberg-style Rauchbier, which means "smoke beer" in German, is made by drying malt over an open flame to impart a smoky character. While other countries produce Smoked Beer, the Rauchbiers of Bamberg, Germany are most known. These beers have a detectable to prevalent smoky character, and most have a low to moderate hop bitterness. Colors and styles of Rauchbier range from light straw Helles or Märzen to dark brown Bock.

Rauchbier

Try it

Aecht Schlenkerla Fastenbier
Brauerei Heller-Trum

Adelscott
Brasserie Fischer

Bishop Bob's Holy Smoke
Dragonmead Microbrewery

Calumet
Brasserie Bièropholie

Eisenbahn Rauchbier
Eisenbahn Brewery

Felsentrunk
Brauerei Gasthof Hartmann

Rauch
Viking Brewing Company

Rauch Bier
Redoak Boutique Beer Café

Rauchbier
Braucommune Freistadt

Rauchbier
Sly Fox Brewing Company

Saranac Rauchbier
The Matt Brewing Company

Smoke Ale
Rogue Ales

Smoked Black Lager
Craftsman Brewing Company

Spezial Rauchbier Lager
Brauerei Spezial

Z Lager
The Fort Collins Brewery

Serve at 50-55° F
Serve in Stange

Serve with

Naturally, smoked meats and cheeses are the most logical and satisfying pairing for a Rauchbier. Good matches include barbequed, grilled, or smoked beef, pork, salmon, or wild game. Smoked cheeses, such as smoked Gruyère, smoked Cheddar, smoked Gouda, and Rauchkäse, make great pairings for Rauchbier.

Rauchbier Marinated Pork

This smoky beer marinade can also be used for pork ribs or rack of lamb. Don't forget to wash it down with a creamy Rauchbier.

2 medium onions, diced
17 oz. Rauchbier
1 tsp. pepper
1 tsp. ground caraway
1 tsp. salt
1 (2 lb.) pork roast
4 carrots, peeled

In a 9″ x 13″ baking dish or large casserole dish, combine onions and beer. Add pepper, caraway, and salt; mix well. Add pork roast to marinade, cover, and refrigerate for 24 to 32 hours, turning a few times. Preheat oven to 450°. Place baking dish in oven and roast for 1 to 2 hours, or to desired doneness, basting 30 minutes with pan juices. Meanwhile, cut carrots into long thin strips and boil in a pot of water (Rauchbier can be substituted in place of water), until tender but still crisp. Slice roast and serve with carrots.

Smoked Salmon on Rye

To round out this meal, pour a glass of Rauchbier and serve chips and coleslaw on the side.

1 (6 oz.) can smoked salmon
½ onion, diced
1 stalk celery, diced
1 tomato, diced
1 carrot, shredded
¼ C. pickle relish
½ C. mayonnaise
1 tsp. salt
1 tsp. pepper
8 slices rye bread, toasted

In a small bowl, combine salmon, onion, celery, tomato, carrot, relish, mayonnaise, salt, and pepper; mix well. Divide mixture evenly onto four slices of toast. Top with remaining four slices to form sandwiches.

According to a diary entry from a passenger on the *Mayflower*, the pilgrims made their landing at Plymouth Rock, rather than continue to their destination in Virginia, due to a lack of beer. Other historians, however, say landing in Plymouth Rock was intentional for other reasons: the abundance of cod, and the area's location outside the control of the Virginia colony.

Potato Cakes

Gruyère performs double duty as it holds these cakes together and highlights the smoky character of the beer.

1 lb. small baking potatoes, unpeeled
1 C. shredded smoked Gruyère
2 large eggs, beaten
1 green onion, thinly sliced
1 tsp. prepared mustard
½ tsp. salt
¼ tsp. pepper
1 T. vegetable oil

Cook whole potatoes in boiling water until tender, about 20 minutes; drain and cool slightly. Peel potatoes and roughly mash in a large bowl. Add Gruyère, eggs, green onion, mustard, salt, and pepper. Mix until well blended. With wet hands, form mixture into ½″ thick patties, 3″ in diameter. Heat oil in a large skillet over medium-high heat. When oil is hot, fry patties, a few at a time, until golden brown on both sides.

Glazed Ham

Smoked ham and smoked beer are a match made in heaven.

1 (12 lb.) fully-cooked smoked ham
1 C. brown sugar
4 tsp. dry mustard
3 T. apple cider vinegar
¼ C. whole cloves

Preheat oven to 325°. If necessary, trim fat from ham, leaving ¼″ layer. Score fat into a diamond pattern across surface. In a medium bowl, combine brown sugar, dry mustard, and vinegar. Stir into a paste and spread over top and sides of ham. Stud center of each diamond with a clove. Place ham in a shallow roasting pan and cover with foil. Bake, basting occasionally, for 15 to 20 minutes per pound, or until a meat thermometer reads 140°F. Remove foil during last 30 minutes of baking time. Let ham stand for 20 minutes before carving.

Porter

American-style Porter is an adapted form of English Porter. American brewers have taken this style to a new level with various methods, including highly hopping the brew, adding coffee or chocolate to complement the burnt flavor, using smoked malts, or aging the beer in barrels. This beer style is dark brown to brownish black with a wide hop bitterness, yet balanced finish.

Porter

Try it

Anchor Porter
Anchor Brewing Company

Black Butte Porter
Deschutes Brewery

Blackhook Porter
Redhook Ale Brewery

Bully! Porter
Boulevard Brewing Company

Caramel Porter
The Matt Brewing Company

Dean's Beans Coffeehouse Porter
Berkshire Brewing Company Inc.

Edmund Fitzgerald Porter
Great Lakes Brewing Company

Mocha Porter
Rogue Ales

New World Porter
Avery Brewing

Porter
Bell's Brewery, Inc.

Porter
Sierra Nevada Brewing Company

Saint Bridget's Porter
Great Divide Brewing Company

Smoked Porter
Alaskan Brewing Company

Stone Smoked Porter
Stone Brewing Company

Stovepipe Porter
Otter Creek Brewing

Serve at 50-55° F
Serve in Stem Glass

Serve with

Pair roasted meats, blackened fish, and smoked sausages with an American-style Porter. Cow's milk cheeses, such as semi-soft Tilsit or hard smoked Gruyère, are a good match for this dark beer style. For dessert, choose rich combinations like chocolate and peanut butter, or toasted coconut and mocha.

Blackened Catfish

A Southern dish full of Creole spice is the perfect thing to stand up to a dark Porter.

2 tsp. cayenne pepper
2 tsp. lemon pepper
2 tsp. garlic powder
2 tsp. salt

2 tsp. pepper
1 lb. catfish fillets
2 T. butter, melted
1 C. Italian dressing

Preheat oven to 350°. In a shallow bowl, combine cayenne pepper, lemon pepper, garlic powder, salt, and pepper. Brush butter over both sides of fillets, then rub generously with seasonings. Heat a large skillet over medium-high heat. Once skillet is very hot, sear fillets for 2 minutes on each side; arrange in a single layer in a lightly greased medium baking dish. Brush dressing over fish; bake for 30 to 35 minutes, or until fish flakes easily with a fork.

———————————————•———————————————

Garlic Rib Roast

Just like an American-style Porter, this herbed roast is flavorful and hearty.

1 (4 lb.) boneless beef
  rib roast
2 cloves garlic, thinly sliced
1 tsp. salt

½ tsp. pepper
½ tsp. dried basil
½ tsp. dried parsley
½ tsp. dried marjoram

Cut 15 to 20 slits in roast, making a few cuts on each side. Insert one slice of garlic in each slit. In a small bowl, combine salt, pepper, basil, parsley, and marjoram; rub all over roast. Place roast, fat side up, on a rack in a roasting pan. Bake, uncovered, for 2 to 2½ hours or until meat reaches desired doneness on a meat thermometer (145°F for medium-rare, 160°F for medium, 170°F for well-done).

Interesting Beer Facts:

- *In the U.S., a barrel contains 31 gallons of beer.*
- *The first beer cans were produced in 1935.*
- *The average American consumes 23.1 gallons of beer annually.*
- *More beer is consumed in America on the 4th of July than any other day.*

Sweet & Sour Sausage

This dish is fragrant and full of smoked flavor. Serve over rice or with mashed potatoes.

1½ lbs. smoked sausage,
   cut into 1″ pieces
1 onion, thinly sliced
1 green bell pepper, seeded
   and cut into long strips
1 red bell pepper, seeded
   and cut into long strips

2 T. butter
Salt and pepper to taste
2 T. sweet and sour sauce
Pinch of cayenne pepper
Dash of hot pepper sauce

Sauté sausage in a large skillet over medium-high heat for 5 to 10 minutes or until well browned. Drain fat from the skillet and set sausage aside. In same skillet, sauté onion and peppers in butter for 10 minutes. Add sausage and mix well; season with salt and pepper. Stir in sweet and sour sauce, cayenne pepper, and hot pepper sauce. Reduce heat to low and simmer for 5 to 10 minutes.

Hot Fudge Dessert

Not only is this dessert rich, decadent, and the perfect thing to stand up to a dark Porter, but it's also incredibly easy to make.

1 (16 oz.) can chocolate
   syrup
¾ C. peanut butter
19 ice cream sandwiches

1 (12 oz.) tub whipped
   topping
1 C. salted peanuts

Heat chocolate syrup in a medium microwave-safe bowl in microwave for 2 minutes; do not allow to boil. Stir in peanut butter until smooth; let cool to room temperature. Line bottom of a 9″ x 13″ baking dish with half of the ice cream sandwiches. (Cut one sandwich in half. Place one full sandwich and one half sandwich along short side of pan. Arrange eight sandwiches in remaining space.) Spread half of the whipped topping over sandwiches, then top with half of the chocolate sauce. Sprinkle with half of the peanuts. Repeat layers. Place in freezer for 1 hour, or until firm. Cut into squares and serve immediately.

Robust Porter

With a more robust flavor than an American-style Porter, Robust Porter is very smooth, deep brownish garnet, with a distinctive character of roasted malts and dark sugars. With high alcoholic strength, Robust Porter, dubbed Baltic Porter, was historically made to withstand being shipped across the North Sea.

Robust Porter

Try it

Baltika 6 Porter
Pivzavod Baltika

Black Boss Porter
Boss Browar Witnica S.A.

D. Carnegie & Co. Porter
Carlsberg Sverige

Gonzo Imperial Porter
Flying Dog Brewery

Hoogstraten Poorter
Brouwerij Sterkens

Imperial Porter
Southampton Publick House

Imperial Porter
Thomas Hooker Brewing Company

Nefarious Ten Pin
Ska Brewing

Okocim Porter
Browar Okocim S.A.

Ølfabrikken Porter
Ølfabrikken

Porteris
Aldaris

Sinebrychoff Porter
Oy Sinebrychoff Ab

Smuttynose Robust Porter
Smuttynose Brewing Company

The Duck-Rabbit Porter
The Duck-Rabbit Craft Brewery

Zywiec Porter
Heineken International

Serve at 50-55° F
Serve in Stem Glass

Serve with

German, Russian, and Lithuanian cuisine often pair well with a complex Robust Porter, especially hearty, smoked meat or wild game dishes. Serve with earthy cheeses, such as Camembert or fontina. Apple pie, pecan pie, cheesecake, chocolate, and other rich spiced desserts taste great with this beer style.

Camembert Bread

Serve these cheesy bread slices as an appetizer, or just as something to nibble while enjoying your favorite Robust Porter.

1 loaf French bread
½ C. butter
4 oz. Camembert cheese,
  cubed

1 T. minced onion
½ tsp. dried basil
½ tsp. salt

Preheat oven to 350°. Slice bread in half horizontally. In a medium saucepan over medium heat, combine butter, cheese, onion, basil, and salt; cook and stir for 5 minutes, or until cheese is completely melted. Spread melted sauce on both cut sides of loaf. Press sides together, wrap in foil, and bake for 15 minutes. Unwrap foil to expose top of bread; bake for 5 more minutes, or until golden. To serve, cut bread into 2″ slices.

Baked Goose

A roasted-flavored Robust Porter complements this recipe of seasoned dark goose meat.

1 whole wild goose, cleaned
1½ tsp. salt
1½ tsp. pepper
1 T. sugar
1 T. cinnamon

1 T. ground ginger
½ C. cider or white wine
  vinegar
½ C. extra-virgin olive oil
¾ C. sherry wine

Preheat oven to 450°. In a small bowl, combine salt, pepper, sugar, cinnamon, and ginger; rub over entire goose. In a separate bowl, combine vinegar, oil, and sherry. Place goose in a roasting pan, breast side down. Pour liquid over goose; cover and bake for 40 minutes. Take lid off roasting pan and broil goose for 8 minutes. Turn goose over and broil for another 8 minutes.

With almost 50 microbrew outlets, Portland, Oregon has more breweries and brewpubs per capita than any other city in the United States. In addition, the Portland-Metro area has the most breweries per capita of any city in the world.

Kugelis

Perfect for matching with a Robust Porter, this baked potato pudding is a Lithuanian national dish. Instead of sour cream, it can also be served with apple sauce or additional crumbled bacon.

5 lbs. red potatoes, peeled
1 large onion, diced
1 lb. bacon, diced
8 eggs
2 T. cornmeal

1 (12 to 14 oz.) can
  evaporated milk
½ C. butter, melted
Salt and pepper to taste
Sour cream

Preheat oven to 400°. Grate potatoes into a large bowl; do not drain. In a medium saucepan, sauté onion and bacon until onion is tender and bacon is slightly crisp; drain grease. Add sautéed mixture, eggs, cornmeal, evaporated milk, butter, salt, and pepper to bowl with potatoes; mix well. Pour potato mixture into a greased 9˝ x 13˝ baking dish; bake for 15 minutes. Decrease oven temperature to 350° and bake for an additional hour, or until browned. Cut into squares and serve with a dollop of sour cream.

Caramel Pecan Pie

Robust Porter has a pleasant acidic flavor, making it a great match for this very rich dessert.

36 individual caramels,
  unwrapped
¼ C. butter
¼ C. milk
¾ C. sugar

3 eggs
½ tsp. vanilla extract
¼ tsp. salt
1 C. pecan halves
1 (9˝) unbaked pie crust

Preheat oven to 350°. In a medium saucepan over low heat, combine caramels, butter, and milk; heat and stir until melted and smooth. Remove from heat and set aside. In a large bowl, combine sugar, eggs, vanilla, and salt. Gradually mix in melted caramel, then stir in pecans; pour into pie crust. Bake for 45 to 50 minutes, or until pastry is golden brown. Let cool until filling is firm.

Sweet & Oatmeal Stout

Sweet Stout, or Cream Stout, has less roasted bitter flavor than other Stouts, plus a full body and sweetness from the addition of unfermented sugars. Oatmeal Stout includes oatmeal in its grist, resulting in a pleasant, smooth body. Both beer styles are very dark with a caramel-like, chocolate-like, coffee-like, or nutty malt character.

Sweet Stout • Oatmeal Stout

Try it

Barney Flats Oatmeal Stout
Anderson Valley Brewing Company

Cream Stout
St. Peters Brewery Ltd.

Ipswich Oatmeal Stout
Mercury Brewing Company

Kalamazoo Stout
Bell's Brewery, Inc.

Milk Stout
Lake Louie Brewing Company

Milk Stout
Lancaster Brewing Company

Milk Stout
Left Hand Brewing Company

Mother's Milk
Keegan Ales

Oatmeal Stout
Goose Island Beer Company

Oatmeal Stout
Samuel Smith's Brewery

Snowplow Milk Stout
Widmer Brothers Brewing Company

St-Ambroise Oatmeal Stout
McAuslan Brewing

The Poet: Oatmeal Stout
New Holland Brewing Company

Too Cream Stout
Dark Horse Brewing Company

Wild Goose Oatmeal Stout
Wild Goose Brewery

Serve at 50-55° F
Serve in English Pint

Serve with

Rich and spicy foods, such as barbequed beef, dishes
with Mexican mole sauce, or fiery Szechuan cuisine, are
appropriate for a Sweet or Oatmeal Stout. Some say a full
farmer's breakfast, complete with eggs, potatoes, meat,
and toast, is the perfect pairing for an Oatmeal Stout. You
can never go wrong when pairing this beer style with
strong earthy French cheeses or thick chocolatey desserts.

Szechuan Beef Satay

The turmeric and cumin in this spicy skewered dish give it authentic Indian flavor. A Sweet or Oatmeal Stout will calm the spice and highlight the flavor.

24 (6″) wooden skewers
¾ lb. strip or fillet steak
¾ C. soy sauce, divided
2 tsp. crushed red pepper flakes, divided
⅛ to ¼ tsp. turmeric powder

1 T. honey
½ tsp. ground cumin
6 T. butter, divided
1 green onion, minced
2 cloves garlic, minced
1 C. chicken broth

Soak skewers in cold water and refrigerate for 1 hour. Cut steak into 24 pieces, each 3″ long by 1″ wide. Slide each piece accordion-style onto a skewer; set aside in refrigerator. In a small bowl, combine ½ cup soy sauce, 1 teaspoon red pepper flakes, turmeric, honey, and cumin; pour over meat, turning to coat all sides; let sit for 15 minutes. Preheat an oven broiler to high, or an outdoor grill to medium-high heat and lightly oil the grate. In a small skillet, melt 2 tablespoons butter. Add green onion and garlic; sauté for 2 minutes. Add chicken broth, remaining soy sauce, and remaining red pepper flakes; heat for 2 more minutes. Strain sauce into a separate skillet and whisk in remaining butter until melted. Broil steak skewers for 30 seconds to 1 minute on each side, or grill for 2 minutes on each side, or until medium-rare. Serve steak skewers with sauce.

Saint-Nectaire Tart

Saint-Nectaire is a French semi-soft cow's milk cheese with a slightly nutty flavor and grassy aroma. Serve this dish as an appetizer or digestif.

7 oz. Saint-Nectaire cheese, thinly sliced
1 (9″) unbaked pie crust
1 large tomato, thinly sliced
Salt, pepper, and cayenne pepper to taste

¼ C. dry bread crumbs
8 Kalamata olives, pitted and sliced
2 T. butter, melted

Preheat oven to 375°. Arrange cheese slices along bottom of pie crust; top with tomato slices. Sprinkle with salt, pepper, cayenne pepper, bread crumbs, and olives; drizzle with butter. Bake for 20 to 30 minutes, or until crust is golden.

Chocolate Espresso Cookies

These cookies and a Sweet Stout share similar chocolate and coffee flavors, which makes for a tasty match.

3 (1 oz.) squares
   unsweetened chocolate
2 C. semi-sweet chocolate
   chips, divided
½ C. butter
3 eggs

1 C. sugar
2¼ tsp. finely ground
   espresso beans
¾ C. flour
½ tsp. baking powder
1 C. chopped walnuts

Preheat oven to 350°. Grease two baking sheets or line them with parchment paper. In a double boiler over simmering water, heat unsweetened chocolate, 1 cup chocolate chips, and butter; stir until melted. In a large bowl, beat eggs and sugar until thick and light, about 3 minutes. Stir in ground espresso and melted chocolate mixture. Sift flour and baking powder into mixture; fold in nuts and remaining chocolate chips. Drop dough by tablespoonfuls 2″ apart on prepared baking sheets. Bake for 10 to 12 minutes. The cookies will crackle slightly when done. Cool for 10 minutes on baking sheets before removing to wire racks to cool completely.

Dark Chocolate Almond Fudge

Rich and creamy – perfect for serving with a nutty-flavored Oatmeal Stout.

4 C. sugar
½ C. butter
1 (12 to 14 oz.) can
   evaporated milk
16 oz. high-quality dark
   chocolate, coarsely
   chopped

1 (7 oz.) jar marshmallow
   cream
1 C. slivered almonds,
   chopped
1 tsp. vanilla extract

Line a 9″ x 13″ baking sheet with foil, extending foil up and over the edges. Lightly grease foil; set aside. In a large saucepan over medium heat, combine sugar, butter, and evaporated milk. Heat, stirring occasionally, until mixture comes to a full boil. Continue to heat until mixture reaches 234°F on a candy thermometer. Remove from heat and gradually stir in chocolate until melted. Fold in marshmallow cream until well mixed, then stir in almonds and vanilla. Spread fudge in prepared pan. Let cool completely, then cover and refrigerate until hardened.

Dry Stout

1759   1959

DRY STOUT

★ ★ ★ ★
Brewed in
Ireland

Classic Irish-style Dry Stout has an initial malt and light caramel flavor with a distinctive dry-roasted bitterness in the finish, usually from the use of coffee-like roasted barley and a generous amount of hops. Velvety-black Dry Stout is low in carbonation and often preserved on a nitro system to achieve a creamy effect.

Dry Stout

Try it

Beamish Irish Stout
Beamish & Crawford Plc.

Black 47 Stout
Old Nutfield Brewing Company, Ltd.

Black Cat Stout
The Portsmouth Brewery

Black Fly Stout
Gritty McDuff's Brewing Company

Bluefin Stout
Shipyard Brewing Company

Dry Stout
Boulevard Brewing Company

Guinness Draught
Guinness Ltd.

Murphy's Irish Stout
Murphy Brewery Ireland

O'hara's Celtic Stout
Carlow Brewing Company

Onward Stout
Yazoo Brewing Company

O'Reilly's Stout
Sly Fox Brewing Company

Out of Bounds Stout
Avery Brewing

Riley's Stout
Paper City Brewing Company

Snake Chaser Irish Style Stout
Lakefront Brewery, Inc.

Three Feet Deep
Furthermore Beer

Serve at 50-55° F
Serve in Stein

Serve with

Hearty yet rich cuisine, such as steak dishes, smoked salmon, meat pies, or beef stew, can stand up to a Dry Stout. Danish blue cheese, French Brie, Dubliner Cheddar, and other strong European cheeses will enhance the beer. For dessert, choose chocolate and coffee combinations, such as tiramisu or mocha mousse.

Oysters on the Half Shell

Oysters and Dry Stout have had a long association, probably beginning with the Irish pubs that commonly served oysters. In fact, oysters occasionally have been used in the brewing process of stout, and there are several Oyster Stouts still in existence. Be sure to only buy oysters that are tightly closed, or purchase oysters that have already been shucked.

2 lbs. oysters
Lemon juice or hot
  pepper sauce

Salt and pepper

Scrub oysters with a stiff brush under running water. So as not to cut yourself, wrap a towel around half of the oyster and hold tightly in palm. Working over a bowl, hold oyster with flatter side facing up. Insert a paring knife between the shells near hinge; twist knife to detach muscles. Remove top shell and scrape meat from top shell into bottom shell. If desired, sprinkle each oyster with lemon juice, hot pepper sauce, salt, and/or pepper.

Irish Cheddar Ball

Spread over rye crackers for a nice complementing flavor to a Dry Stout.

4 oz. cream cheese, softened
½ tsp. Dijon mustard
1 clove garlic, minced
1 T. Dry Stout

1 C. shredded Irish Cheddar
  cheese
1 T. chopped fresh parsley
½ C. chopped black olives

In a medium bowl, mix together cream cheese, mustard, garlic, beer, Cheddar cheese, parsley, and olives. Mix well, then shape into a log or ball. Refrigerate to harden. Remove from refrigerator 30 minutes prior to serving.

Beef & Mushroom Stew

Seasoned with Dry Stout, this stew is hearty and packed with flavor.

2 lbs. cubed beef
Flour
3 T. butter, divided
2 T. sunflower or vegetable
  oil, divided
2 medium onions, roughly
  chopped
1 C. button mushrooms
10 to 12 oz. Dry Stout

2 T. tomato paste
1 T. sugar
1 bay leaf
2 sprigs fresh thyme
2 sprigs fresh parsley
1 sprig fresh rosemary
Salt and pepper to taste
8 oz. shiitake mushrooms

Preheat oven to 325°. Toss beef lightly in flour. Heat
1 tablespoon butter and 1 tablespoon oil in a large skillet
over medium-high heat; brown beef in batches, then transfer
to a large casserole dish. Add another 1 tablespoon butter
and 1 tablespoon oil to skillet; sauté onions until lightly
browned. Add button mushrooms to skillet and heat just
until softened. Transfer onions and mushrooms to casserole
dish. Pour beer into skillet and bring to a boil, stirring to
loosen any bits from bottom of skillet. Stir in tomato paste
and sugar, mixing until dissolved; pour over ingredients in
casserole dish. Add enough water to cover ¾ of the meat,
making sure not to cover meat entirely. Tie together bay leaf,
thyme, parsley, and rosemary sprigs with kitchen twine; add
to casserole dish. Season stew with salt and pepper; cover
dish and place in oven. Cook for 2 to 3 hours, or until meat
is very tender, stirring occasionally. If necessary, add a little
hot water during cooking time. Remove and discard stalks
from shiitake mushrooms. Slice caps thickly and sauté in
remaining butter in skillet. Stir mushrooms into stew and
return to oven for 5 more minutes. Discard herbs and ladle
stew into bowls.

Guinness, an Irish Dry Stout, is known to be high
in iron content. Hospital patients in England, as
well as blood donors, used to be given Guinness post-
operation. In Ireland, Guinness is still available to blood
donors, and sometimes offered to stomach and intestinal
post-operative patients.

Imperial Stout

Russian-style and American-style Imperial Stout, called the king of stouts, boasts a high alcohol content and plenty of malt character. This beer style is black in color and very robust. American-style Imperial Stout tends to have a higher, cleaner alcohol flavor, a higher hop level, and more residual malt sweetness than Russian-style.

Imperial Stout

Try it

Big Bear Stout Ale
Bear Republic Brewing Company

Black Chocolate Stout
Brooklyn Brewery

Blackout Stout
Great Lakes Brewing Company

Breakfast Stout
Founders Brewing Company

Dragonslayer Imperial Stout
Middle Ages Brewing Company

Imperial Stout
Berkshire Brewing Company Inc.

Imperial Stout
Moylan's Brewery

Old Heathen
Weyerbacher Brewing Company

Old Rasputin X Imperial Stout
North Coast Brewing Company

Siberian Night
Thirsty Dog Brewing Company

Speedway Stout
AleSmith Brewing Company

Storm King Stout
Victory Brewing Company

The Abyss
Deschutes Brewery

World Wide Stout
Dogfish Head Craft Brewed Ales

Yeti Imperial Stout
Great Divide Brewing Company

Serve at 50-55° F
Serve in Snifter

Serve with

This beer style easily overpowers most main dishes, so choose foods carefully. A few dishes, however, are hearty enough to compete: dark, smoked meats or foie gras, for example. Long-aged cheeses, such as Gouda, Parmesan, or Cheddar, make good matches. For dessert, serve rich dark chocolate truffles, mousse, or cheesecake. You may find, though, that a dark Imperial Stout is really a meal in itself and pairs well with an after-dinner cigar.

Macaroni & Aged Cheddar

Long-aged Cheddar is sharp and strong enough to stand up to an Imperial Stout, making for a great dinner combination.

8 oz. uncooked macaroni
3 eggs, beaten
1½ C. shredded aged
  Cheddar cheese

1½ C. milk
½ tsp. salt
1 T. Worcestershire sauce
Dash of hot pepper sauce

Preheat oven to 325°. Bring a large pot of lightly salted water to a boil. Add macaroni and cook until tender but still firm, stirring occasionally; drain and place in a large lightly greased casserole dish. In a medium bowl, combine eggs, cheese, milk, salt, Worcestershire sauce, and hot pepper sauce; mix well. Pour over pasta. Bake for 40 to 45 minutes.

Chocolate Caramel Squares

Caramel and chocolate flavors are taken to a new height when enhanced by a robust Imperial Stout.

1 (14 oz.) pkg. individual
  caramels, unwrapped
1 (12 to 14 oz.) can
  evaporated milk, divided
1 (18 oz.) pkg. German
  chocolate cake mix

⅔ C. butter, melted
¾ C. chopped walnuts
  or pecans
1 (12 oz.) pkg. semi-sweet
  chocolate chips
1 C. shredded coconut

Preheat oven to 350°. In a saucepan over medium heat, combine caramels and ¼ cup evaporated milk. Heat, stirring constantly, until caramels are melted and smooth; keep warm over low heat, stirring occasionally. In a medium bowl, combine cake mix, butter, nuts, and remaining evaporated milk. Spread half of the mixture in an ungreased 9″ square baking dish; bake for 6 minutes. Sprinkle chocolate chips and coconut over baked layer. Drizzle with caramel, then top with remaining batter. Bake for 10 minutes, or until cake portion is slightly dry to the touch.

Chocolate Truffles

The epitome of rich dessert, these truffles should be savored while sipping on an Imperial Stout.

10 oz. bittersweet chocolate, finely chopped
3 T. unsalted butter
½ C. heavy cream
1 T. light corn syrup
¼ C. brandy

½ C. cocoa powder, finely chopped nuts, and/or toasted coconut
8 oz. semi-sweet chocolate, finely chopped

Melt bittersweet chocolate and butter in a microwave-safe bowl in microwave for 30 seconds; remove and stir, then microwave for 30 more seconds and stir again. In a small saucepan over medium heat, combine heavy cream and corn syrup; heat until simmering and pour over melted chocolate mixture. Let stand for 2 minutes. Using a rubber spatula, stir gently, starting at middle and stirring in a circular motion until all chocolate is melted. Stir in brandy. Pour mixture into an 8″ square glass baking dish; refrigerate for 1 hour. Using a melon baller, scoop chocolate balls onto a parchment-lined baking sheet; return to refrigerator for 30 minutes. Spread cocoa powder, nuts, and/or coconut on separate plates; set aside. Meanwhile, line a large bowl with a heating pad set to medium. Place another bowl over heating pad; add semi-sweet chocolate. Heat chocolate, stirring occasionally, until it reaches 90° to 92°F, without exceeding 94°. Remove truffles from refrigerator and roll gently between palms into a round shape. Dip an ice cream scoop in melted chocolate, then turn upside down to remove any excess. Place one truffle in scoop and roll around until coated in chocolate. Coat truffle with cocoa powder, nuts, or coconut. Leave truffle in coating for 15 seconds, then remove to a parchment-lined baking sheet. Repeat until all truffles are coated. Let cool for 1 hour, then store in an airtight container in refrigerator. Serve at room temperature.

For centuries, beer was brewed without hops. It was flavored with herbs such as rosemary and thyme until it was discovered that hops helped preserve beer and prevent it from spoiling. Hops have now become a vital part of beer's aroma and flavor.

Fruit Beer

Fruit beers are made in a wide range of beer styles using fruit or fruit extracts for an obvious, yet harmonious, fruit aroma and taste. The fruit qualities may be added in the mash, kettle, primary, or secondary fermentation, and they should not be overpowered by hop character. Characters of acidic fermentation may be evident to contribute to and enhance the fruity balance.

Fruit Beer

Try it

#9
Magic Hat Brewing Company

Aprihop
Dogfish Head Craft Brewed Ales

Bar Harbor Blueberry Ale
The Atlantic Brewing Company

Blackbeary Wheat
Long Trail Brewing Company

Blue Paw Wheat Ale
Sea Dog Brewing Company

Éphémère
Unibroue

Orange Blossom Cream Ale
Buffalo Bill's Brewery

Pete's Wicked Strawberry Blonde
Pete's Brewing Company

Purple Haze
Abita Brewing Company

Rübaeus
Founders Brewing Company

Samuel Adams Cherry Wheat
The Boston Beer Company

Strawberry
Melbourn Bros.

Tres Blueberry Stout
Dark Horse Brewing Company

Wild Raspberry Ale
Great Divide Brewing Company

Wisconsin Belgian Red
New Glarus Brewing Company

Serve at 40-45° F
Serve in Stange

Serve with

Since Fruit Beer is available in many beer styles, it is difficult to name certain foods that are a guaranteed match. Salads with vinaigrette dressings, however, will enhance almost any Fruit Beer. In addition, fruit-based desserts are always a good bet.

Spinach Salad with Raspberries

Match this salad with a raspberry-inspired beer for a flavorful pairing.

3 T. vegetable oil
2 T. raspberry vinegar
2 T. raspberry jam
⅛ tsp. pepper
8 C. torn fresh spinach
½ C. thinly sliced onion

2 C. fresh raspberries,
  divided
4 T. slivered almonds,
  toasted, divided
3 kiwis, peeled and sliced
1 C. seasoned croutons

In a jar with a tight-fitting lid, combine oil, vinegar, jam, and pepper; shake well. In a large salad bowl, combine spinach, onion, 1 cup raspberries, and 2 tablespoons almonds; toss until evenly distributed. Drizzle dressing over salad and top with remaining raspberries, almonds, kiwis, and croutons.

Apricot Pasta Salad

You can't go wrong when pairing this salad with an Aprihop (Dogfish Head Craft Brewed Ales) or other stone fruit-flavored beer, such as peach or cherry flavors.

4 oz. fusilli pasta
6 fresh apricots, coarsely
  chopped
1 C. cooked, chopped
  chicken

2 small zucchini, cut into
  thin strips
1 red bell pepper, seeded and
  cut into thin strips
1 T. chopped fresh basil

Bring a large pot of lightly salted water to a boil. Add pasta and cook until tender but still firm, stirring occasionally. Drain pasta and refrigerate until chilled. In a large bowl, combine chilled pasta, apricots, chicken, zucchini, red pepper, and basil; toss until evenly distributed.

A rush for free beer, food, and souvenirs after the coronation of the last Russian emperor, Nicholas II, resulted in the deaths of more than 1,300 people. Four days after his coronation, the emperor held a banquet at Khodynka Field, the town square. After rumors spread that there were not enough beer and gifts for everyone, many people were injured, and hundreds were trampled to death in a mass panic now known as the Khodynka Tragedy.

Blackberry Cobbler

A good food pairing for many beer styles, this dessert is particularly enhanced by berry-flavored beers.

1 C. butter or margarine, softened, divided
1 C. plus 2 T. sugar, divided
1½ C. self-rising flour
⅓ C. milk, room temperature

2 C. fresh or frozen blackberries
½ tsp. ground cinnamon

Preheat oven to 350°. Melt ½ cup butter and place in a 10″ round or oval baking dish; set aside. In a saucepan over medium-high heat, combine 1 cup sugar and 1 cup water, stirring until sugar is completely dissolved; set aside. Place flour in a mixing bowl. Using a pastry blender, cut remaining butter into flour until fine crumbs form; add milk and stir with a fork until a dough forms. Turn dough out onto a lightly floured surface; knead four times, then roll into a 9″ x 11″ rectangle, ¼″ thick. Spread berries and cinnamon over dough; roll into a log, then cut into ¼″ slices. Place slices, cut side down, in baking dish. Pour sugar mixture around slices. Bake for 45 minutes. Sprinkle remaining sugar over top and bake for an additional 15 minutes.

Lemon Pie

Serve this pie to boost the citrus notes of any lemon, orange, or lime-flavored beer.

3 T. butter, softened
1¼ C. sugar
4 eggs, separated
3 T. flour
Dash of salt

1¼ C. milk
Grated peel of 2 lemons
⅓ C. fresh lemon juice
1 (9″) unbaked pie crust

Preheat oven to 375°. In a large bowl, cream together butter and sugar until light and fluffy. Beat in egg yolks, flour, salt, milk, lemon peel, and lemon juice. In a small bowl, beat egg whites until stiff. Gently fold whites into lemon mixture. Pour mixture into pie crust. Bake for 5 minutes, reduce temperature to 300° and bake for 45 minutes, or until top is golden.

Pumpkin Beer

Pumpkin Ales and Lagers are made using pumpkin (or cucurbita pepo) as an adjunct in either the mash, kettle, primary, or secondary fermentation. The result is beer with a subtle to intense, yet harmonious, pumpkin quality. These beers are often spiced with other flavorings, though the hop character does not overpower the pumpkin aroma or taste.

Pumpkin Beer

Try it

America's Original Pumpkin Ale
Buffalo Bill's Brewery

Blue Moon Pumpkin Ale
Blue Moon Brewing Company

Cottonwood Pumpkin Spiced Ale
Carolina Beer & Beverage Company, LLC

Great Pumpkin Ale
Cambridge Brewing Company

Ichabod: Pumpkin Ale
New Holland Brewing Company

Imperial Pumpkin Ale
Weyerbacher Brewing Company

Post Road Pumpkin Ale
Brooklyn Brewery

Pumking
Southern Tier Brewing Company

Pumpkin Ale
Southampton Publick House

Pumpkin Beer
O'Fallon Brewery

Pumpkin Patch Ale
Wild Goose Brewery

Pumpkinhead Ale
Shipyard Brewing Company

Punkin Ale
Dogfish Head Craft Brewed Ales

Saranac Pumpkin Ale
The Matt Brewing Company

Smuttynose Pumpkin Ale
Smuttynose Brewing Company

Serve at 45-50° F
Serve in English Pint

Serve with

Often a seasonal brew, Pumpkin Beer is a great match for autumn foods and flavors. Dishes including apples, squash, cranberry, caramel, sage, cloves, or nutty flavors make a great match. In addition, roasts, hot sandwiches, hearty soups, pumpkin desserts, or fruit pies will all enhance the flavor of a Pumpkin Beer.

Autumn Snack Mix

The flavors of fall fill up this snack mix and are ready to highlight similar spices in a Pumpkin Beer.

½ C. butter or margarine
⅓ C. honey
¼ C. brown sugar
1 tsp. ground cinnamon
½ tsp. salt
3 C. sweetened square
  oat cereal

1½ C. old-fashioned oats
1 C. chopped walnuts
½ C. dried sweetened
  cranberries
½ C. chocolate-covered
  raisins

In a medium saucepan over medium heat, combine butter, honey, brown sugar, cinnamon, and salt; heat, stirring often, until butter is melted and sugar is completely dissolved. In a large bowl, combine cereal, oats, and walnuts; drizzle with butter mixture and toss. Place mixture on a greased jellyroll pan and bake for 45 minutes, stirring every 15 minutes. Remove from oven and let cool for 15 minutes before stirring in cranberries and raisins. Store in an airtight container.

Sweet Potato Chowder

Flavored with Pumpkin Beer, this chowder is great on a cool October day.

2 lbs. sweet potatoes, diced
8 C. chicken broth
2 onions, finely diced
2 (15 or 16 oz.) cans sweet
  potatoes, drained

1 tsp. salt
24 oz. Pumpkin Ale
1 lb. smoked bacon, cooked
  and crumbled

Preheat oven to 450°. Arrange diced sweet potatoes in an even layer on a 9˝ x 13˝ baking sheet. Roast potatoes in oven for 20 minutes, or until tender. Meanwhile, in a medium soup pot over medium heat, combine chicken broth, onions, and canned sweet potatoes. Heat for 30 minutes, stirring frequently. Reduce heat to low and let simmer, stirring to break up sweet potato. Add salt, beer, and bacon; heat for an additional 30 minutes, stirring frequently. Stir in roasted sweet potatoes and heat for an additional 15 minutes. If chowder is too thick, stir in more beer and heat for an additional 10 minutes.

Apple & Walnut Dessert

Scoop a helping of this warm dessert into a bowl and top with a scoop of vanilla ice cream. Pumpkin Beer has met its match!

8 C. peeled, cored, and
  sliced tart apples
2 tsp. ground cinnamon
2¼ C. brown sugar, divided
1 C. butter or margarine,
  softened

2 eggs
2 C. flour
1 C. finely chopped walnuts,
  divided

Preheat oven to 350°. Place apples in a greased 9″ x 13″ baking dish; sprinkle with cinnamon and ¼ cup brown sugar. In a medium bowl, cream together butter and remaining brown sugar. Add eggs, then stir in flour and ½ cup walnuts; spread over apples. Sprinkle with remaining walnuts. Bake for 45 to 55 minutes, or until apples are tender.

Pumpkin Bread Pudding

To serve this tasty bread pudding, just top with a dollop of whipped cream and pair with a Pumpkin Beer.

8 oz. French bread, torn
  into small pieces
2 C. half n' half
3 large eggs
⅔ C. sugar
⅔ C. brown sugar
1 (15 oz.) can pumpkin
  puree

1 C. dried cranberries
3 T. butter, melted
1 tsp. ground cinnamon
½ tsp. ground nutmeg
½ tsp. ground ginger
1 tsp. vanilla

Preheat oven to 350°. Place torn bread in a large bowl; pour half n' half over top; set aside. In a separate bowl, combine eggs, sugar, brown sugar, pumpkin, cranberries, butter, cinnamon, nutmeg, ginger, and vanilla; mix well. Pour pumpkin mixture over soaked bread, stirring to blend. Pour mixture into a greased 7″ x 11″ baking dish. Bake for 45 to 60 minutes, or until set.

Herbed & Spiced Beer

Herbed or Spiced Beer has a distinct aroma and flavor derived from roots, seeds, fruits, vegetables, or flowers used in the brewing process. Under-hopping is a technique often used to allow the herbs or spices to contribute to the beer's profile without being overtaken by hops or malts used in the beer. Though the herbs and spices cannot always be identified, most contribute to a balanced flavor.

Herbed • Spiced Beer

Try it

Black Wattle Superior
Barons Brewing Company

Chateau Jiahu
Dogfish Head Craft Brewed Ales

Crop Circle
Hop Back Brewery

Frederick Miller Classic Chocolate Lager
Miller Brewing Company

Gingerbread Ale
Bison Brewing Company

Hoppy Holidaze
Marin Brewing Company

Island Ginger
The Atlantic Brewing Company

JuJu Ginger
Left Hand Brewing Company

Juniper Pale Ale
Rogue Ales

Midas Touch Golden Elixir
Dogfish Head Craft Brewed Ales

Nicie Spicie
Short's Brewing Company

Passover Honey Lager
Ramapo Valley Brewery

Poor Richard's Tavern Spruce
Yards Brewing Company

Saranac Winter Wassail
The Matt Brewing Company

Vanilla Porter
Breckenridge Brewery

Serve at 45-50° F
Serve in Dimpled Mug

Serve with

Be creative with food pairings for an Herbed or Spiced
Beer. Think in terms of known dishes that have benefited
from the addition of a certain herb or spice. For example,
cinnamon-like flavors work well with apples, nuts,
breads, and baked goods. Try pairing these foods with
a cinnamon-flavored beer.

Smoked Salmon Maki Roll

Serve this sushi roll with a ginger-flavored beer for a familiar combination.

2 C. cooked sushi rice
6 T. rice wine vinegar
6 sheets nori seaweed sheets
2 T. wasabi paste
1 cucumber, peeled and cut
  into long thin strips

1 avocado, peeled, pitted,
  and finely cubed
8 oz. smoked salmon, cut
  into long strips

Preheat oven to 300°. Immediately after rice is cooked, mix in rice wine vinegar. Spread rice onto a plate until completely cooled. Place nori sheets on an ungreased baking sheet. Heat in oven for 1 to 2 minutes, or until warm and pliable. Center one nori sheet on a bamboo sushi mat. Wet hands and spread a thin layer of rice over nori, pressing down lightly. Dot some wasabi paste over rice; top with a row of cucumber, avocado, and salmon down center of rice. Lift the end of the mat and roll it over the ingredients, pressing gently. Roll forward to make a complete roll. Repeat with remaining nori sheets and ingredients. Use a wet, sharp knife to cut each roll into four to six pieces.

Spiced Pecans

Serve these spiced nuts warm with a chilled Christmas-inspired beer, such as Hoppy Holidaze (Marin Brewing Company) or Saranac Winter Wassail (The Matt Brewing Company).

1 egg white, lightly beaten
3 C. pecan halves
½ C. sugar
½ tsp. salt

1 tsp. ground cinnamon
½ tsp. ground cloves
½ tsp. ground nutmeg

Preheat oven to 350°. Line a baking sheet with foil; set aside. In a small bowl, beat egg white with 1 tablespoon water; stir in pecans until well moistened. In a separate bowl, combine sugar, salt, cinnamon, cloves, and nutmeg; sprinkle over nuts, tossing until coated. Spread nuts on prepared pan. Bake for 30 minutes, stirring every 10 minutes.

Ham Balls

Present these as an appetizer or main dish with a honey-flavored beer for a sweet combination!

2 lbs. fully-cooked
  ground ham
1 lb. ground beef
1 lb. ground pork
2 C. graham cracker crumbs
2 eggs, beaten
⅔ C. milk

1 (10.75 oz.) can tomato
  soup
½ C. brown sugar
2 T. honey
2 T. vinegar
1 T. ground mustard

Preheat oven to 350°. In a large bowl, combine ham, beef, pork, crumbs, eggs, and milk; mix well and shape into 48 balls. Place ham balls in two greased 9˝ x 13˝ baking dishes. In a medium bowl, combine soup, brown sugar, honey, vinegar, and ground mustard; pour over ham balls. Bake, uncovered, for 45 to 50 minutes, basting every 10 minutes with sauce.

Gingersnaps

These cookies are a great accompaniment for molasses-flavored beer.

1 C. brown sugar
¾ C. shortening
¼ C. molasses
1 egg
2¼ C. flour
2 tsp. baking soda

1 tsp. ground cinnamon
1 tsp. ground ginger
½ tsp. ground cloves
¼ tsp. salt
⅓ C. sugar

In a medium bowl, beat together brown sugar, shortening, molasses, and egg. Stir in flour, baking soda, cinnamon, ginger, cloves, and salt; cover and refrigerate for 1 hour. Preheat oven to 375°. Shape dough into rounded teaspoonfuls of dough; dip tops into sugar. Place, sugared side up, on greased baking sheets. Bake for 10 to 12 minutes, or until set. Remove cookies to wire racks to cool.

The act of collecting beer mats and coasters is known as "tegestology". A person who does so is called a "tegestologist".

My Beer & Food Pairings

Use this page to record your successful (or not-so-satisfying) beer and food pairings. Then, rate each pairing on a scale of 1 to 10.

The beer:_____

The food:_____

Tasters:_____

When served:_____

Rate the pairing: 1 2 3 4 5 6 7 8 9 10

The beer:_____

The food:_____

Tasters:_____

When served:_____

Rate the pairing: 1 2 3 4 5 6 7 8 9 10

The beer:_____

The food:_____

Tasters:_____

When served:_____

Rate the pairing: 1 2 3 4 5 6 7 8 9 10

The beer:_____

The food:_____

Tasters:_____

When served:_____

Rate the pairing: 1 2 3 4 5 6 7 8 9 10

The beer:_____

The food:_____

Tasters:_____

When served:_____

Rate the pairing: 1 2 3 4 5 6 7 8 9 10